"The heaventree of stars hung with humid nightblue fruit."

—James Joyce, *Ulysses*

Exotic Fruit:
Mother Nature's *second* best reason to get a little sticky.

—Norman Van Aken

THE GREAT
Exotic
Fruit
BOOK

A HANDBOOK OF TROPICAL AND SUBTROPICAL FRUITS, WITH RECIPES

NORMAN VAN AKEN
WITH **JOHN HARRISSON**

PHOTOGRAPHY BY
LOIS ELLEN FRANK

1⊃
TEN SPEED PRESS

↑☻

Ten Speed Press
Box 7123
Berkeley, California 94707

Text and cover design by Nancy Austin
Based on posters designed by Barbara Flores
Photographs by Lois Ellen Frank
Photographs of guanabana (page 31) and mangosteen (page 49)
    by Mark Schechter
Photograph of rambutan (page 67) by Larry Schokman
Food and location photography on pages ii, vi, 78, 95, 98, 108, 126,
    and back cover by Greg Schneider
Illustrated border by Julie Cohn
Lettering by Lilly Lee

Library of Congress Cataloging-in-Publication Data

Van Aken, Norman, 1951-
    The exotic fruit book : a guide to tropical and subtropical fruits
  / Norman Van Aken with John Harrisson.
        p.   cm.
    Includes bibliographical references.
    ISBN 0-89815-688-2 :
    1. Cookery (Tropical fruit)   2. Tropical fruit.   I. Harrisson, John.
II. Title.
  TX811.V35   1995
  641.6'46—dc20   94-49370
                                                        CIP

Printed in Korea

1 2 3 4 5 6 7 8 9 10 — 99 98 97 96 95

This book is dedicated to Grandpa Ray, a man who was the best adopted Grandpa anyone could ever hope for. Thank you for sharing your unbelievable garden, orchards, and time with us. Time passes, but the fruit is falling, luscious still.

＊　＊　＊

SPECIAL THANKS TO

Larry M. Schokman, Assistant Director of the Kampong, of the National Tropical Botanical Garden, Coconut Grove, Florida.

Dr. Jonathan H. Crane, Tropical Fruit Crops Specialist, University of Florida, IFAS Tropical Research and Education Center, Homestead, Florida.

Marsha Sayet

And thanks for your generosity to:
>   Brooks Tropicals, Homestead, Florida
>   Frieda's Inc., Los Angeles
>   Mauna Loa Macadamia Nut and
>   Royal Kona Coffee, Honolulu, Hawaii
>   Mark and Kiki Ellenby
>   Chris Rollins
>   Murray Corman
>   Dr. Bob Knight
>   Robert Moehling
>   Bill Hopkins
>   Adolph Grimal
>   William O. Lessard
>   Robert Barnum
>   Bill Schafer
>   Stephanie Johnson
>   Robin Sprague
>   Mitchell Kaplan
>   Tony Merola
>   Joan Green
>   Mario Martinez
>   Noble Hendrix
>   Julie Cohn

CONTENTS

Introduction 1

GUIDE TO EXOTIC FRUIT 5

Acerola 6
Akee 6
Asian Pear 8
Atemoya 8
Avocado 10
Florida Avocado 10
Cocktail Avocado 10
Babaco 12
Banana 14
Finger Banana 14
Red Banana 14
Bignay 16
Black Sapote 16
Breadfruit 18
Calomondin 18
Canistel 20
Cherimoya 20
Ciruela 22
Citron 22
Clementine 22
Coconut 24
Coffee 24
Date 26
Durian 26
Feijoa 28
Fig 28
Grapefruit 30
Guanabana 30
Guava 32
Imbé 32
Jaboticaba 34
Jakfruit 34
Kiwano 36
Kiwi Fruit 36
Kumquat 38
Langsat 38
Lemon 38

Mexican or Key Lime 40
Persian or Tahiti Lime 40
Longan 42
Lychee 42
Macadamia Nut 44
Mamay Sapote 44
Mamoncillo 46
Mango 46
Mangosteen 48
Melon 48
Miracle Fruit 50
Monstera 50
Muscadine Grape 52
Orangequat 52
Papaya 54
Green Papaya 54
Passion Fruit 56
Pepino 58
Persimmon 58
Pineapple 60
Plantain 62
Hawaiian Plantain 62
Pomegranate 64
Prickly Pear 64
Pummelo 66
Rambutan 66
Sapodilla 68
Sour Orange 68
Star Fruit 70
Sugar Apple 70
Tamarillo 72
Tamarind 72
Unique Fruit 74
Velvet Apple 74
Wampi 76
Wax Jambu 76
White Sapote 76

BEVERAGES 79

Shocking Pink Limeade 80

Puckery Prickly Pear Limeade 81

Batido Exótico 82

Bahama Mama Mamey Milk Shake 83

Tamarind Twister 84

Preserve of Six Citrus Fruits with Five Spice Powder 85

A Sun-Burned Rum Runner 86

Sapodilla Root Beer Float (a.k.a. The Tropical Black Cow) 88

SOUPS, STARTERS, & SALADS 89

Chilled Exotic Fruit Soup 90

Double Fruit Cocktail "Straight Up" 91

Jamaican Red Banana and Peanut Fritters with an
Orange Marmalade, Horseradish and Scotch Bonnet Jam 92

Cherimoya-Avocado Salad with Crispy Chinese Chicken,
Roasted Cashew Nuts and a Passion Fruit Dressing 94

Mixed Greens and Fruits Salad with Toasted Pistachios
and Warm Loxahatchee Chevre 96

MAIN DISHES 99

Key West Sweet Plantain Stuffed and Spiced
Pork Tenderloin with a Sour Orange Marinade 100

Fish and Fruit "Port of Call" 102

Pomegranate Molasses Marinated and Grilled
Lamb Chops with a Pomegranate-Lamb Jus 104

Ancho Chile and Guava Glazed Smoked Ham 106

SALSAS, CHUTNEYS, CONDIMENTS, & PRESERVES 109

All-Purpose Exotic Fruit Salsa 110

Bajan Avocado Cocktail Salsa 111

Exotic Fruits Curry 112

Pineapple-Scotch Bonnet Mojo 113

Pawpaw Pickle Tartar Relish 114

Sweet and Sour Jaboticabas with
Fire Roasted Pearl Onions 115

Pepino, Mango, and Asian Pear Slaw 116

East Indian Spiced Fruit Yogurt 117

Horned Melon Raita 118

Homemade Key Lime Mustard 119

Pineapple and Sugarcane Moonshine Chutney 120

SIDE DISHES 121

Tropical Tuber French Fries and Mango-Tamarind Ketchup . . . 122

Arroz con Coco Oriente 124

Pummelo Juice Couscous 125

BRUNCH, BREADS, & DESSERTS 127

Star Fruit Flapjacks 128

Mamey Sapote and Cuban Sweet Potato Waffles 129

Jamaican Banana-Pineapple Rum Bread 130

Deep Dish Asian Pear Pie 131

Hot Guanabana-Lime Soufflé 132

Fruit Salsa Speckled Sweet Pizza Pie
with a Red Tamarillo Sauce 134

Rum Caramel-Espresso Poached "Niño" Banana Splits 136

Creamy, *But Frozen* Passion 137

Canistel "Egg Nog" Ice Cream 138

Mango Cinnamon Sorbet 139

Candied Kumquat Key Lime Pie 140

West Indian Pumpkin Pound Cake with
Monstera Mash Anglaise 142

SOURCES 144

CONVERSION CHART 145

INDEX 146

x

✦ ✦ ✦

INTRODUCTION

For hundreds of thousands of years, mangoes have fallen in Asia. For who knows how long, children in the Andean highlands of Peru have urgently tugged a cherimoya apart to taste the sweet, perfumed delicacy of this treasure. From time immemorial, coconuts have floated across the South Seas, washing up on far-flung beaches.

Fruit—natural, no additives, low fat, heart-smart, good for you. With every day that passes, exotic fruits—like their great counterpart, chiles—increasingly are working their way into our lives. Just as North Americans have found a friend in the fire of chiles due to their embrace of Mexican, South American, Caribbean, Thai, Indian, and Chinese cuisines (among others), so tropical and subtropical fruits are another indispensible and common ingredient that figures dramatically in the cooking of these regions.

Our demographic map in North America is changing as we approach the new century. The pattern of immigration has changed, with the old, predominantly European influx being replaced by heavily Latin and Asian migrations, thus broadening our cultural and culinary choices as we interface with our new neighbors. We are seeing all kinds of exotic fruits that these communities are bringing with them, and their popularity is crossing into the main-stream. The word "exotic" is derived from the Latin root, "exo," meaning "out of." Thus the primary meaning of exotic is "coming from another country."

As we eat in ethnic restaurants, we are learn-ing the differences in the foods of Cuba and

Jamaica, Korea and Thailand, in just the same way we learned to distinguish between the refinement of Northern Italian cuisine and the robust flavors of Southern Italy. The way these cultures approach their native exotic fruit is refreshingly different. For example, a common generalization about Asian cuisine is that desserts play an insignificant role; however, some kind of sweet refreshment in the form of exotic fruit is often eaten after the meal. Unadorned purity. Our neighbors from the Caribbean and South America eat fruit desserts too, but they also have a long tradition of drinking a wide variety of fruit drinks; *jugos* (juices) and *batidos* (fruit shakes) abound in tropical markets.

In both ethnic and mainstream fruit and vegetable markets, we are seeing new fruits appear next to familiar standbys. Just as the banana and pineapple have been everyday fruits since the 1950s, so the kiwi, pomegranate, and mango have become instantly recognizable during the last twenty years. More recently, we have seen cherimoyas, pepinos, and horned melons in our stores, and in talking to exotic fruit experts and suppliers, it is clear that these are just the initial drops in a torrent that is about to sweep us. The mamey sapote, mangosteen, rambutan, and durian, popular and prized in their respective homelands, cannot be far away from Main Street availability and acceptance.

This book will help you learn what some of these fruits look like (inside and out), where they come from, how they taste, and how you can use them. Following their descriptions, you will find over forty recipes that give examples of how to cook some of the fruits identified.

My personal discovery of these fruits began when I moved to the island of Key West in 1971. The little Cuban restaurants I frequented had big colorful signs advertising the batidos made with sapodilla, tamarindo, mamey sapote, atemoya, and so on. I was nineteen years old, and everything seemed so exotic. "Am I still in America?" I wondered. It was another reason to fall in love with the place (a feeling that still beats strong). I began tasting these fruits, cautiously and haltingly at first, and moved on to buying them in the markets, growing in confidence as my experience broadened.

As time passed, as I started to get more and more into professional cooking, I began to introduce some of these exotic fruits into dishes in both traditional and innovative ways. I enjoyed using pan-cooked sweet plantains as an orthodox accompaniment for Roast Pork Havana, or giving beurre blanc a tropical twist by adding sweet plantains to match grilled spiny lobster. I soon became known for this type of cooking. In the mid to late 1980s, I developed a "New World Cuisine" style of fusion cooking that used exotic fruits as a significant element, and a growing number of my colleagues in South Florida were simultaneously cooking in the same fashion. This was our way of responding to our environment and the resources available to us, just as the pioneers of Southwestern or Californian cuisine were products of local circumstances and product availability. Exotic fruit played an important role in establishing the style and flair of the New World Cuisine.

In 1991, I took my family "up the road" from the Florida Keys to Miami, where my experiences continued to be inspired by the increasing availability of exotic fruits. Here we have the Tropical Fruit and Spice Park, The Fairchild Tropical Gardens, The Kampong (a sort of living tree and fruit museum), Brooks Tropicals, and many more growers and suppliers, especially in the Redlands area. These are to South Florida what Napa Valley is to Northern California. The care, nurturing, and knowledge

that these institutions and the individuals concerned
bring to the subject matter has accelerated my
understanding and appreciation for fruit in count-
less ways.

As I travel around the country, I am always
able to find local markets that can supply the different exotic fruits I need to recreate my dishes for
special dinners. Invariably, I will meet the owner of
one of these markets, an employee, or a customer,
and we'll strike up a conversation that will give me
some additional insight into the nature or availability of these marvelous fruits. I have even learned
that many of these exotic fruits are becoming available in Europe, sometimes in the unlikeliest places.
And so it came about that Ten Speed Press/Celestial
Arts invited me to create the Exotic Fruits posters,
dividing the rich subject matter into two posters,
by tropical and subtropical classification. This divi-
sion is a useful rule of thumb, if not conclusive, as
some subtropical fruit prosper in tropical conditions
and vice versa, and others do well in temperate
climates. This book includes this information, but
is not organized along those lines, taking instead an
alphabetical approach.

When I spot a group of people clustered in
front of my Exotic Fruits posters in a store, it gives
me unique pleasure to see them reacting to them.
This is especially true if it happens to be a mixed
group, pointing to and touching the images and
speaking in different languages or accents about the
fruits, their different names, the memories they
inspire, the dishes, the flavors. It is then that I real-
ize what those posters and this book are all about.
It is about sharing the Earth's bounty, ever evolving
and broadening and unfolding. Take some time to
see, touch, smell, and taste the wonderful sweetness
and richness that are being offered.

Guide to Exotic Fruit

Some tropical fruits prosper in subtropical climates and vice versa. Likewise, some subtropical fruits will grow in temperate climates. The tropical/subtropical classifications included in this book refer to the conditions in which the fruits are most productive, or in which they are most commonly found.

Most of the fruit depicted is from two-thirds to three-quarters of actual size, with the exception of the jakfruit, melon, pepino, and pineapple which are roughly half size.

ACEROLA
(BARBADOS CHERRY)

(Malpighia glabra)

TROPICAL

Cherry-like fruit grows on a decorative shrub-like tree. Sweet to acidic, juicy, pink to red flesh; flavor a little like tart strawberries. Exceptionally rich in vitamin C content (twenty to fifty times that of an orange); just one or two of these will supply a whole day's vitamin C needs. Sweet varieties mostly eaten fresh, when fully ripe; also used for preserves and juice. Native to the Caribbean and Central America; also grown in Florida, Central and South America. Available spring through fall.

AKEE
(OR ACKEE)

(Blighia sapida)

TROPICAL

Timing is everything: immature and overripe fruit are poisonous. Fruit that has fallen from the tree should never be eaten. The pink material that connects the (edible) aril to the seeds must be removed as it can cause illness. For all these reasons, therefore, the akee is not imported nor commercially grown in the United States. However, the delicately flavored akee is very popular in Jamaica, where it is traditionally eaten sautéed with butter and codfish, or on toast; it tastes very much like scrambled eggs. Native to West Africa but commonplace in the Caribbean, especially Jamaica (Captain Bligh introduced it there, hence the Latin name). Fruit of a handsome decorative evergreen tree.

ASIAN PEAR
(CHINESE OR SAND PEAR; APPLE PEAR; NASHI)

(Pyrus Pyrifolia)

SUBTROPICAL

These apple-size pears often seem to grow surprisingly—and almost perfectly—round. The speckled yellow or green skin probably accounts for their alternative name of Sand Pear.

Firm, crisp, juicy white flesh with crunchy texture like an apple and a sweet flavor somewhat like a pear. Mostly eaten fresh or used as a garnish—they can be sliced extremely thin and not crumble or tear. Good in salads, also when stewed and slightly chilled. Substitute for apples or pears. Native to China and Japan, where they are grown extensively. Available late summer and early fall.

ATEMOYA

(Annona atemoya, hybrid)

TROPICAL

Man-made hybrid of the cherimoya and sugar apple (sweetsop). Heart-shaped or round fruit with pale green, easily-bruised, bumpy skin. Juicy, smooth, white flesh is a little sweet and a little tart, tasting like a piña colada without the alcohol! Numerous inedible black seeds throughout the flesh.

Eaten fresh (best chilled), and used in fruit salads, fruit drinks, and desserts. Native to South and Central America. Also grown commercially in Florida, Hawaii, California, New Zealand, and Australia. Available late summer through early winter.

AVOCADO
(ALLIGATOR PEAR)

(Persea Americana)

SUBTROPICAL

There are three types of avocado: Mexican, Guatemalan, and West Indian. The pear-shaped Haas (pictured at top), grown widely commercially, is a Guatemalan/Mexican hybrid. Avocados ripen after they are picked.

Delicate buttery/nutty flavor; pale yellow-green flesh has a smooth texture. Avocados have a relatively high fat content (monounsaturated oil). Delicious eaten fresh and used for guacamole, salads, soups, desserts, and as garnish. Native to Central and South America (the name is derived from the Aztec word, *ahuacatl*). Available year-round.

FLORIDA AVOCADO

(Persea Americana)

SUBTROPICAL

Guatemalan/West Indian hybrid (also known as Choquette variety, pictured at center). Smooth skinned and much larger than the California varieties (such as the Haas avocado). Contains less oil and fat than the Haas, and as with other avocados, it contains no cholesterol. Same uses as the regular avocado. Native to Central America.

COCKTAIL AVOCADO

(Persea Americana)

SUBTROPICAL

Seedless fruit (miniature Fuerte variety) resembling a thin gherkin or pickle. Smooth green skin and pale green flesh with a creamy consistency. Eaten fresh as a snack and used for salads, soups, and garnish.

BABACO
(MOUNTAIN PAPAYA)

(Carica pentagona)

SUBTROPICAL

Related to the papaya and grows on similar, unusual-looking trees. Five-sided (hence the Latin name); skin turns golden when completely ripe. Cream-colored seedless flesh is aromatic and juicy, with a slightly acidic, tropical fruit flavor. Sometimes compared with melon in texture and flavor. Eaten fresh when fully ripe, used for its juice, and in preserves, chutneys, fruit salads, and desserts. Native to the South American Andes, now grown extensively in New Zealand.

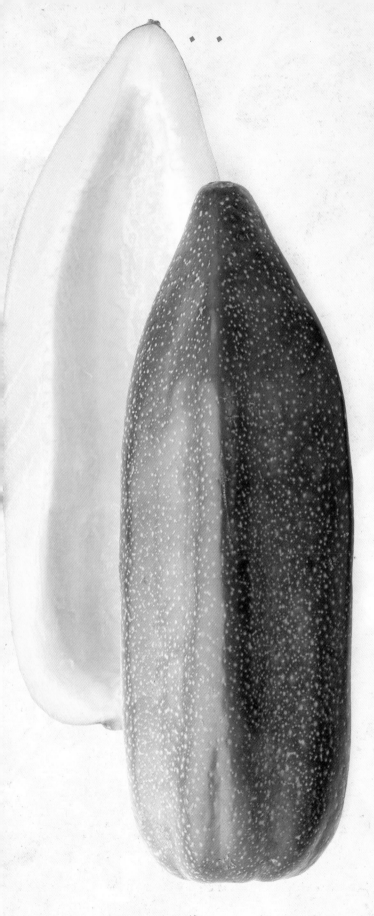

13

BANANA

(Musa Paradisiaca)

TROPICAL

The banana plant is a fast-growing giant herb, the fruit of which was almost unknown in the United States until the end of the nineteenth century. Modern commercial varieties include the Cavendish (Chinese), Brazilian, and Bluefields. Very nutritious; high in mineral and vitamin content.

Highly versatile—can be eaten ripe or cooked, in desserts, fruit salads, breads, and drinks. Native to Southeast Asia (although the name is from West Africa). Available year-round.

BANANA, FINGER
(LADY FINGER; DWARF; NINO; DATIL)

(Musa Accuminata)

TROPICAL

There are many varieties of this banana, which is a miniature version of the regular banana. Must be fully ripe to yield the best flavor, which is more concentrated and sweeter than regular bananas. Uses similar to regular bananas. Native to Southeast Asia.

BANANA, RED
(INDIO; CUBAN RED; MORADO; JAMAICAN RED; MACABOO)

TROPICAL

Two varieties grown in the East Indies are called Adam's Fig Tree and Paradise Banana, which helps perpetuate the Muslim belief that bananas were the true "forbidden fruit" of Eden and that the First Couple used banana skins to conceal their nakedness. Smaller in size than regular bananas. Creamy white to pink flesh, with a strong flavor. Usually eaten raw. Native to Southeast Asia.

BIGNAY

(Antidesma Montanum)

SUBTROPICAL

Small, round or oval fruit grows in grape-like clusters. Thin-skinned with white pulp. High in vitamin A content. Fully ripe fruit has slightly sweet, sub-acid flavor, while immature fruit tastes astringent, rather like cranberries. Used for desserts, preserves, and high-quality homemade wine. Native to the Phillipines, India, Southeast Asia, and also grown in Florida. Available late summer through fall.

BLACK SAPOTE
(BLACK PERSIMMON, CHOCOLATE PUDDING FRUIT)

(Diospyros digyna)

TROPICAL

Green-skinned fruit of an ornamental evergreen; related to the persimmon. High in vitamin C. Chocolate-brown flesh (hence the alternative name) and a sweet, rich flavor. Ripens quickly, when it becomes very soft. Eaten fresh with lemon juice or a little vanilla; used for preserves and in breads and desserts, especially ice cream and mousse. Native to Mexico, and grown in South Florida, the Caribbean, Hawaii, and California. Available fall through spring.

BREADFRUIT

(Artocarpus altilis, A. incisus)

TROPICAL

Average about nine to twelve inches around. The knobbly green skin (which develops a brown or yellowish tint as it ripens) is separated into five-sided segments. Slightly fibrous, white to yellow bland-tasting flesh that sweetens (and becomes less starchy) as the fruit ripens.

A highly adaptable table food. Breadfruit, along with other sources of starch such as taro, cassava, and sweet potatoes, has long been an important staple throughout the tropics. Only edible when cooked; mostly eaten like potatoes. Mashed with cream and butter, also makes excellent chips. Sometimes used for soup, stew, bread, or pudding. Native to Southeast Asia. Cultivated in the Pacific Rim region for thousands of years and introduced to the Caribbean by Captain Bligh. Available mostly July through February.

CALOMONDIN

(Citrus mitis)

SUBTROPICAL

The fruit grows on small, spiny shrub-like trees. This miniature orange-like citrus fruit probably is related to the orangequat; others speculate it may be a naturally-pollenated cross between the kumquat and mandarin orange. It is sometimes confused with the kumquat, but tastes more tart (rather like a lemon). The thin peel is also edible. Used mostly for juice, sauces, and preserves; can be used as a substitute for lemon. Native to China, grown extensively in the Philippines, also in Florida and Hawaii.

CANISTEL
(YELLOW SAPOTE; EGG FRUIT)

(Pouteria campechiana)

TROPICAL

New cultivars have improved flavor and texture. Egg yolk or eggnog richness gives this fruit its alternative name, but the oval, pointed fruit must be fully ripe for the rich flavor to fully develop. The orange flesh has a somewhat mealy texture if eaten before it is fully ripe. Addictively pleasurable, it is mostly eaten fresh with a spritz of citrus juice; also used in drinks (especially milk shakes or batidos), custards, ice creams and desserts. Cultivated by the pre-Columbian civilizations of Central and South America. Available mostly in summer and fall.

CHERIMOYA
(CUSTARD APPLE)

(Annona cherimola)

SUBTROPICAL

Name derived from the Quechua (Incan) word *chir-imuya,* or "cold seeds," and grows up to altitudes of 6,000 feet. Should be stored at room temperature. Pine cone or heart-shaped, highly perfumed, with a thick, shingled, pale green rind. Inside, the creamy white delicate flesh contains a variable number of large inedible black seeds. Soft, smooth texture with an intense, uniquely delicious sweet flavor with banana, vanilla, mango, and pineapple tones. Mostly eaten fresh, best when slightly soft and chilled. Also used for salads, sauces, drinks, desserts, and ice cream. Native to Central and South America; culti-vated widely in Australia, New Zealand, Spain, and Israel. Mostly available in the winter. Related to the atemoya, sugar apple, and guanabana.

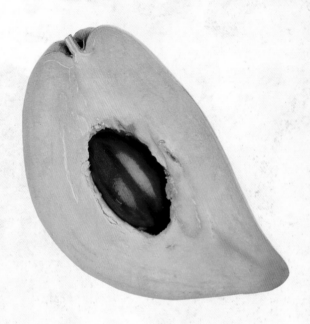

CIRUELA
(PEANUT BUTTER FRUIT)

(Bunchosia Armeniaca)

TROPICAL

Grows on shrubs or trees that bear several crops of fruit a year. Skin is red or orange, flesh is cream-colored or red. Alternative name because of sweet, peanut-butterlike flavor; some astringency. Mostly eaten fresh, also used for preserves. Native to South America, also grown in South Florida.

CITRON

(Citrus medica)

TROPICAL

Citrus fruit that resembles a lumpy oversized lemon. The pulp is very acidic and unsuitable for eating. Cultivated mainly for its very thick, aromatic rind, which is candied and used for preserves and desserts. The rind is also pressed for oil used to flavor liqueur. Native to China, and grown widely in the Mediterranean and Puerto Rico.

CLEMENTINE
(MANDARIN ORANGE)

(Citrus reticulata)

SUBTROPICAL

Tiny loose-skinned orange with thin peel and tangy red-orange flesh. Easy to peel and usually with few or no seeds. High in vitamin C. Sweet and juicy, with concentration of orange flavors. Mostly eaten fresh. Cultivated mostly in Spain, Morocco, and Algeria. Available November through May.

COCONUT

(Cocos nucifera)

TROPICAL

One-seeded fruit of the coastal coco palm. A true king of tropical fruit because of its versatility. There is a South Seas saying that, "He who plants a coconut tree plants food and drink, vessels and clothing, a source of heat, habitation for himself and a heritage for his children."

Inside the nut is the edible part of the fruit. Before it ripens, the fruit's flesh at this stage of maturity is known as "water coconut," which is jellylike and can be eaten with a spoon. On maturity, the flesh solidifies and becomes crisp to form "coconut meat"; this is kept moist by the thin, opaque coconut juice. The juice (and coconut "milk," pressed from the meat), is used as a drink, for sauces and curries, or puddings and desserts; the flesh used mainly for sauces and desserts. Dried flesh (copra) also used for desserts and for oil. The most widely cultivated palm, native to Southeast Asia. Available year-round.

COFFEE

(Coffea arabica)

SUBTROPICAL

The ripe, red berry of the evergreen shrub-like coffee plant, the coffee "cherry," must be picked by hand as the fruit ripens at different times on the same plant. The "cherries" are pulped, sun-dried and hulled to yield two green beans each. The dried beans are always roasted before being ground and used for drinking or as a dessert flavoring. Occasionally used in sauces, such as red-eye gravy.

Native to the uplands of Ethiopia. The largest producers in the world are Brazil and Colombia. Also grown extensively in Central America and the Caribbean. Available year-round.

DATE

(Phoenix dactylifera)

SUBTROPICAL

The fruit of the date palm has a thin, papery skin and very sweet, sticky flesh. Fresh dates are yellow, golden brown, or black, but are more commonly available semi-dried, when they are brown. Eaten fresh, semi-dried, and dried, and used in desserts and confectionery. Native to the Middle East, where it has been cultivated for thousands of years, especially as a desert oasis fruit. Also grown in North Africa, and to a lesser extent, in California and Arizona. Semi-dried and dried dates available year-round.

DURIAN

(Durio zibethinus)

TROPICAL

The fruit of this evergreen tree is covered with a dull, green, spiny, semi-hard shell. Inside, the sweet yellow flesh is deliciously rich and juicy with a custard-like consistency. The shell of some varieties exudes an unpleasantly strong, fetid odor, making it (to some) the "bad boy" of the fruit world! Even airlines and most hotels have banned it, making it difficult to obtain in the United States.

Eaten fresh or chilled, used in ice cream and desserts, or cooked with rice. The chestnut-flavored durian seeds can be cooked. Native to Malaysia and Indonesia, where it is highly prized; some consider it an aphrodisiac. Rich in protein.

FEIJOA
(PINEAPPLE GUAVA)

(Feijoa sellowiana)

SUBTROPICAL

The egg-shaped fruit of an ornamental evergreen tree. In the same family as guava (Myrtaceae—the myrtle family), and shares a similar flavor. Strongly scented (almost musky), with tones of pineapple, strawberry, lime, and mint. When slightly soft and ripe, the creamy white to yellow flesh is smooth but crisp, rather like the texture of a pear, and a little tart in flavor. Small edible seeds. Eaten fresh or used in fruit salads, preserves, and sauces. Native to South America. Mostly grown commercially in New Zealand. Available spring through fall.

FIG

(Ficus carica)

SUBTROPICAL

A staple of ancient Mediterranean civilizations. Held sacred by some, and symbolizing peace and prosperity for others. At least 600 varieties, in shades of white, purple, green, and red. Thin-skinned and round or pear-shaped. The flesh ranges from white to red, with a soft, juicy texture and a sweet, nut-like flavor. Highest sugar content of any fruit. Eaten fresh and dried; also used for baking and in desserts. Available canned. Native to the Mediterranean and the Middle East (Asia Minor). Available year-round; peak season in summer.

GRAPEFRUIT

(Citrus paradisi)

SUBTROPICAL

Grow in clusters, resembling grapes, hence the name. High in vitamin C. Rind varies, from thin to very thick; flavor varies from mildly acidic to tart. Pink and yellow fruit available year-round; red-fleshed varieties (ruby grapefruit) available mainly in fall and winter months. Eaten fresh and used for juice, salads, and preserves. Originated in the West Indies (Jamaica) as a mutation or hybrid of the pummelo during the eighteenth century. Grown extensively in California, Texas, Florida, and Arizona.

GUANABANA
(SOURSOP)

(Annona muricata)

TROPICAL

Delicious! Heart-shaped fruit of an evergreen tree with thin, leathery dark green skin covered with soft spines. White, pulpy, juicy, aromatic flesh with a slightly acidic flavor. Some liken the flavor to that of banana. The seeds are toxic. Grown for its pulp and juice for drinks; also used in desserts. Native to the American tropics. Related to sugar apple, cherimoya, and atemoya, but up to three times as large. Available year-round.

GUAVA

(Psidium Guajava)

SUBTROPICAL

This round or oval-shaped fruit is classified as a berry and is high in vitamin C. The edible skin is white, yellow, green, or pink in color; the pale yellow variety is often the sweetest. The flesh may be white, yellow, or pink. Different varieties have different flavors; for example, strawberry, lemon, and pineapple. Eaten fresh, used in desserts, and for nectar, juice, preserves, and sauces. Also available canned. Guava wood is popular for grilling because of its intense aroma. Native to the American tropics; grown extensively in Hawaii, California, and Florida as well as Asia and South Africa. Related to the myrtle. The Aztecs called them *xalxocotl* ("sand plum") because of the many small edible pips. Available spring and summer.

IMBÉ

(Garcinia livingstonei)

TROPICAL

Tree mostly grown as an ornamental. Small, brilliant yellowish-orange, thin-skinned fruit with a large seed. The small amount of juicy, edible pulp is pleasantly sweet yet acidic. The juice is notorious for its indelible staining quality. Mostly eaten fresh, also used in drinks.

Native to Mozambique and East Africa; grown in South Florida. Available September through March.

JABOTICABA

(Myrciaria cauliflora)

SUBTROPICAL

The dark purple, grapelike fruit are unusual and spectacular because they grow *directly* from the tree trunk and main branches. The edible, thin but tough skin contains sweet, white, milky pulp with a flavor between grapes and plums. Tiny seeds are edible, but slightly tannic. Eaten fresh and used for desserts, sauces, preserves, and wine. Native to Brazil. Available spring through fall.

JAKFRUIT

(Autocarpus heterophyllus)

TROPICAL

Related to breadfruit and figs; largest tree fruit in the world, weighing up to eighty pounds each! The spiny, knobbly-skinned oval fruit grows directly out of the trunk and branches. When ripe, the lightgreen skin turns yellow or brown and the fruit develops an intense fragrance. Juicy, sweet yellow or pink flesh with tones of melon, mango, and papaya.

Aril surrounding seed eaten fresh and used in desserts; unripe mature fruit cooked as a vegetable. Roasted seeds have a chestnut flavor and are used for seasoning. Native to Malaysia and India, and named by Portuguese explorers after the Malay word for the fruit, *tsjaka.* Grown throughout the tropics as well as South Florida.

KIWANO
(HORNED MELON)

(Cucumis metalicerus)

SUBTROPICAL

Spiky, brilliant golden-orange skin with emerald green flesh. Jelly-like texture with a flavor between banana, watermelon, and cucumber. Best stored at room temperature. Mostly eaten fresh or in slaws. The scooped-out shell makes a dramatic container for a chilled kiwano soup. Native to Africa, grown extensively in New Zealand and California. Available year-round.

KIWI FRUIT
(CHINESE GOOSEBERRY)

(Actinidia deliciosa)

SUBTROPICAL

Was it talent or a cute stage name that made the kiwi fruit the emblem of the Nouvelle Cuisine movement? Nonetheless, the kiwi has withstood the test of time.

Large egg-size fruit grows on fruit vines. The firm, brown skin covered in soft downy hairs contains the brilliant jade-green juicy flesh and attractive, dark, edible seeds. Delicate, sweet and slightly tart flavor that combines banana, peach, and strawberry. Eaten fresh, and used in fruit salads, compotes, ice cream, preserves, and as a garnish. Native to China, but pioneered commercially in New Zealand, hence the name. Also grown in Australia and California. Available year-round.

KUMQUAT

(Fortunella)

SUBTROPICAL

The smallest citrus fruit, averaging 1½ inches around. The round Meiwa kumquat (pictured) is a hybrid of the round and oval (Nagami) kumquats. Sweet, thin edible skin and juicy, tart flesh. Eaten fresh and used in salads, sauces, preserves, and ice cream. Candied, and also bottled in syrup. Native to China; also grown commercially in Japan and the United States. Available in winter months.

LANGSAT

(Lancium domesticum)

TROPICAL

Fruit of an evergreen tree. Oval shaped with thin green skin that turns yellow when ripe. White, translucent aromatic flesh with a sweet-and-sour flavor. Mostly eaten fresh; also used in preserves. Native to Southeast Asia. Available mostly in spring. The duku variety is a large type of langsat.

LEMON

(Citrus limon)

SUBTROPICAL

Bright yellow oval-shaped citrus fruit. Skin varies from thin to thick. Juicy, yellow, acidic flesh. High in vitamin C. Highly versatile; lemon juice is a universal seasoning agent, used especially in desserts, baking, marinades, and drinks. The citric acid in lemon juice preserves the natural color of many foods. Zest also used for cooking and for its oil content. Originally native to India and Asia. Used by the ancient Greeks and Romans. Grown extensively in California. Available year-round.

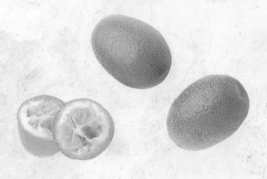

LIME
(MEXICAN, WEST INDIAN, BARTENDER, OR KEY LIME)

(Citrus aurantifolia)

TROPICAL

One of the comestibles that defines Key West (the other is conch) and much in demand from tourists and locals alike. High in vitamin C, and for this reason were eaten by British sailors in the eighteenth century to resist scurvy (which led to the nickname "limey"). Small, round citrus fruit with thin skin that is often a mottled yellow-green. Acidic juice. Commonly used juiced, in cocktails (especially margaritas), with fish, in sauces, salsas, and of course in authentic Key Lime Pie. Native to India and Asia, this species is grown in South Florida, Mexico, and the Caribbean. Available year-round.

LIME
(PERSIAN, TAHITI, OR BEARSS LIME)

(Citrus latifolia)

SUBTROPICAL

Larger than the Key lime, and shaped more like a lemon. Tart, juicy, pale green pulp; less flavorful than the tropical Mexican or Key lime. Thick, fragrant rind. Often used as a substitute for lemon; juice used especially in drinks, preserves, desserts and marinades; pickled; zest also used in cooking and for its oil. Native to Malaysia. Available year-round.

LONGAN
(DRAGON'S EYE)

(Euphoria longana)

SUBTROPICAL

Smaller version of the lychee, native to China and Thailand. Fruit of an ornamental tree. The smooth, leathery light brown skin peels easily. It contains off-white, translucent sweet flesh that has a some-what spicy, musky flavor, with gardenia tones. The black seed is inedible. Texture varies from crisp to soft, and usually, not quite as juicy as the lychee. Typically eaten fresh or in fruit salads. Used in Oriental soups and desserts. Can be frozen in their skins and are available dried and canned. Also grown in South Florida. Available in summer.

LYCHEE
(LITCHI)

(Litchi chinensis)

SUBTROPICAL

The lychee is to a table grape as a haiku is to pop music. Smooth, aromatic, and juicy white flesh inside the thin, rough, slightly spiky and leathery pink to red shell. Small inedible brown seed. Flavor somewhat like muscat grapes; rich in vitamin C. Eaten fresh; used in fruit salads, also bottled, canned, frozen (in their shells) and dried (lychee nuts). Native to eastern China, where it has been cultivated for thousands of years. Also grown in Southeast Asia, Australia, Israel, South Africa, Florida, and Hawaii. Available mainly in mid-summer.

MACADAMIA NUT

(Macadamia integrifolia)

SUBTROPICAL

Originally grown as an ornamental. Smooth, fleshy green husks containing the golden brown hard nut split open when ripe. The nut is exceptionally hard to crack. Inside, the large cream-colored kernel is buttery rich and slightly sweet, and has a high fat content. Eaten raw, or roasted and used in desserts, baking, savory dishes, and for garnish. Also pressed for oil. Native to Australia and named for John Macadam, a Scottish-born Australian chemist who cultivated it. Grown most extensively in Hawaii and on a limited scale in California. Available year-round.

MAMEY SAPOTE
(MAMEY)

(Pouteria sapota)

TROPICAL

Grows on highly ornamental evergreen trees. The skin is somewhere between very soft sandpaper and peach fuzz. Oval-shaped fruit with rich and creamy pink or orangey-red aromatic flesh. The unique, exotic flavor is a mixture of sweet potato, avocado, and honey, which makes it destined to become a prized and popular tropical fruit. Considered by some to be an aphrodisiac. Eaten fresh, and used in milk shakes, soups, preserves, and desserts. Native to Central America. Grown extensively in Mexico, South America and the Caribbean. Available in the summer.

MAMONCILLO
(SPANISH LIME)

(Melicoccus bijugatus)

TROPICAL

Round or oblong, smooth, green fruit of an ever-green tree. Thin leathery peel, with a large ball-like seed or pit. Soft, juicy, white, cream-colored or orange translucent pulp, with a sweet, sub-acid flavor. Eaten fresh and used in drinks. Native to the American tropics.

MANGO

(Mangifera indica)

TROPICAL

More than 500 varieties with different shapes, sizes, colors, and flavors; among the most common are Tommy Atkins, Haden, and Kent. When ripe, the thin skin of many types turns red, orange, yellow, or purple, and the fruit is soft to the touch. The firm, sweet, and exotically perfumed golden-orange flesh must be cut away from the large oval pit or seed. The luscious flesh is very juicy and can be messy to eat (or sensual, depending on your point of view!).

Eaten fresh and used in drinks, desserts, fruit salads, and salsas; green mangoes used in Asian chutneys and slaws. Native to India and Southeast Asia, where it has been cultivated for thousands of years. Grown widely in the tropics and subtropics, including Florida, Hawaii, and California. Available year-round; peak season summer and fall.

MANGOSTEEN

(Garcinia mangostana)

TROPICAL

A delicious and aromatic berry that is sometimes referred to as "Queen of tropical fruits."

Thick purplish-brown hard shell, with soft, white, waxy flesh divided into segments. Delicate texture and a sweet, sub-acid, refreshing flavor. Eaten fresh and used for dessert, especially sorbet. The shell is used for the dye it produces. Native to Malaysia and Indonesia; also grown widely in South America. Unrelated to the mango in any way. Available mostly in the spring and summer, but unfortunately, few are imported into the United States.

MELON
(CHARANTAIS OR FRENCH)

(Cucumis melo)

SUBTROPICAL

Melons are annual trailing herbs and members of the gourd family; related to squash. This is a type of canteloupe or rockmelon. Sweetly perfumed, with golden-orange flesh with plenty of inedible seeds that must be scooped out. Sugary tasting, fragrant flesh. Mostly eaten fresh. Native to the Middle East. Available year-round.

MIRACLE FRUIT

(Synsepalum dulcificum)

TROPICAL

Aptly named because although it has little flavor, it works miraculously and uniquely on the palate to make any sour or acidic flavored fruit or food taste sweet! (It will not make sweet foods taste sweeter, however.) This effect lasts up to thirty minutes.

Fruit of a small evergreen; oval and sized like a red olive. Slightly sweet white flesh. Eaten fresh. Native to West Africa. Available most of the year.

MONSTERA
(CERIMAN OR MEXICAN BREADFRUIT)

(Monstera Deliciosa)

TROPICAL

Resembles a pale green banana or a long cucumber with lizard-like hexagonal platelets or scales that fall off as the fruit ripens, which it does in stages. You can take a knife and gently scrape the ripe fruit away from the cob-like core and eat it in stages until more of it turns ripe.

Lusciously exotic flesh with creamy, custard-like consistency. Sweet acidity, with banana and pineapple flavor tones when ripe. However, if eaten unripe, acidic crystals and unpleasant flavor will irritate the mouth and throat. Eaten fresh or in desserts. Native to Mexico and Guatemala. Also grown in Florida and California.

MUSCADINE GRAPE

(Vitis rotundifolia)

SUBTROPICAL

Thick-skinned with a musky, fruity, yet tannic flavor. Eaten fresh, used for juice, preserves, and desserts. Also made into wine (scuppernong). Native to Florida and the Southeast United States. Available August through October.

ORANGEQUAT

SUBTROPICAL

Man-made hybrid of the satsuma mandarin and the Meiwa kumquat. First described botanically in the 1930s. Thick, spongy mild-flavored peel, and an acidic pulp. Mostly eaten fresh or used for preserves. Available October through December.

PAPAYA
(TREE MELON; PAWPAW; FRUTA BOMBA)

(Carica papaya)

TROPICAL

Columbus called these the "fruit of angels." Fast-growing fruit that develops in clusters, like coconuts, on a tall, single-stemmed herbaceous tree. Large variation in size; the small, yellowish pear-shaped "Solo" variety is the most common in United States markets.

Hard and green in unripe form (see Green Papaya below); ripe when the smooth, inedible skin is a uniform yellow, orange, gold, or rose color. The firm, yellow to rose colored flesh is aromatic and smooth, with exotic flavor tones that include peaches or apricots and berries. The striking, peppery-flavored black seeds are edible, but usually are discarded before eating. Mostly eaten fresh; wonderful with a spritz of lime juice as the flesh lacks acidity. Also used in salsas, salads, smoothies, and desserts. Source of papain, a natural enzyme, tenderizer, and digestive. Native to tropical America; grown extensively throughout the tropics, including Hawaii, and in Florida. Unrelated to the wild North American pawpaw *(Asimina triloba)*. Available year-round; prime season is early summer.

GREEN PAPAYA

(Carica papaya)

TROPICAL

Immature papaya (see above).

Used in Asian-style slaws and salads, and in soups, stews, relishes, and chutneys. Also cooked like squash or vegetable; sometimes stuffed.

PASSION FRUIT

(Passiflora edulis)

TROPICAL

This prolific vine fruit is named for its exotic flower, imaginatively said to resemble the iconography (wounds, nails, crown of thorns, apostles) of the Crucifixion (Christ's "Passion"). To me, the ripe fruit looks like a handball that just had a serious workout on a gravel driveway.

Tough, bumpy, round, or slightly oval-shaped skin. Colored in shades of red, lavender, dark purple, or yellow, it turns wrinkly when ripe. This exterior is in stark contrast to the interior, with its intensely aromatic yellow-green or yellow-orange edible seeds and pulp. Rich and luscious, with a complex and refreshing, sweet-and-sour floral flavor. Eaten fresh, used in sauces, desserts and ice cream, and puréed for juice. Canned nectar is also available. Native to Brazil. The yellow passion fruit (not pictured) is native to Australia. Available virtually year-round.

PEPINO
(MELON PEAR OR TREE MELON)

(Solanum muricatum)

SUBTROPICAL

The fruit of a small herbaceous bush. Fragrant lemon-yellow to golden exterior with vivid purple or violet stripes when ripe. Soft, dense, and juicy sweet yellow flesh with an aroma and flavor like rockmelon or cucumber. Contains inedible seeds. Eaten fresh, in fruit salads and desserts or as a garnish, and also used for its juice. Best spritzed with a little citrus juice. Native to the South American Andes, grown extensively in New Zealand. Available in the winter and spring.

PERSIMMON

(Diospyros kaki)

SUBTROPICAL

Most know of persimmon better as a crayon color than a familiar fruit. This fruit grows on large ornamental deciduous trees; the name comes from the Algonquin Indian language.

Smooth orange, aromatic skin. The flesh has a creamy texture and a tangy, sweet flavor like a cross between plums and pumpkin. Must be eaten fully ripe or tastes astringent because of high tannin levels (at that stage, you may prefer the flavor of the crayon!). Non-tannic, firmer varieties (such as the Fuyu) now increasingly available. Eaten fresh; used in desserts, baked goods, puddings and game sauces, and available dried (an excellent high-energy snack). A tea can be made from the leaves. Native to China and Japan. Available late fall and early winter.

PINEAPPLE

(Ananas Comosus)

TROPICAL

First brought to Europe by Columbus. Named for its (vaguely) pine-cone appearance. The fruit grows on a spiny, agave cactus-like plant (albeit much smaller) that is a herbaceous perennial. The pineapple is a "multiple fruit"—a collective of small, botanically individual fruits that form the whole. This is denoted by the mosaic-like, hexagonal "diamond" patterns that make up the tough, bumpy skin, which is fragrant and yellow when ripe, sometimes mottled with green or brown.

The fruit's yellow or white flesh is very juicy when ripe and can be rather fibrous. Tangy, sweet and tart flavor. Once picked, the fruit's starch does not convert to sugar, so it must be harvested when ripe. Eaten fresh, used in desserts, salads, preserves, and as garnish. Can be cooked. Also used for juice, canned and frozen. Native to Central and South America. Now grown commercially throughout the tropics, and especially in Southeast Asia, Central and South America, and Hawaii. Available year-round.

PLANTAIN
(COOKING BANANA)

(Musa X paradisiaca)

TROPICAL

Larger and wider than the related banana, with thick skin. In unripe form, the skin is green and the fruit hard. As the fruit ripens, the skin turns to yellow, then brown, and at its ripest and softest, a dull licorice-black. Usually peeled with a knife.

Starchy and less sweet than bananas; flavor and texture rather like squash. Used extensively for cooking (as a starch) in the Caribbean, South America and Asia when either green (unripe), brown (semi-ripe) or black (ripe); also makes great chips. Not eaten raw. Native to Southeast Asia. Available year-round.

HAWAIIAN PLANTAIN
(HUA MOA)

(Musa sapientom)

TROPICAL

Excellent texture for cooking. Same uses as regular plantain.

POMEGRANATE

(Punica granatum)

SUBTROPICAL

A member of the berry family. An ancient fertility symbol because it has so many seeds (symbol of the goddess Artemis). Considered sacred or mystical by many civilizations.

Thick, leathery, crimson-to-brown shell contains a pinkish pulp and edible scarlet seeds that are tender, sweet and tart. The seed compartments are surrounded by a cream-colored membrane or pith, which is very bitter and inedible. The red pomegranate juice released by the pulp stains indelibly. Seeds eaten fresh, used in salads, desserts, sorbets, as a garnish, and for juice and in sauces. The juice was originally the main component of grenadine syrup.

Native to the Middle East. Peak season is late fall and early winter.

PRICKLY PEAR
(CACTUS PEAR OR TUNA)

(Opuntia ficus-indica)

SUBTROPICAL

The fruit of the desert cactus (nopales and opuntia varieties) is actually a berry and contains a multitude of crunchy edible seeds. These fruit grow in clusters and have a slightly oblong or egg-shape. The thin spiny thorns should be removed before handling.

Orange, garnet red, or purple skin and flesh when ripe. Watermelon-like aroma and intense flavor; refreshing, firm texture. Allow to ripen at room temperature, and then chill. If the seeds are large, strain them out. Use peeled in salads, sauces, desserts, jams, and jellies. Native to Mexico; also common throughout the Southwest United States and Central America. Peak season is fall and winter.

PUMMELO
(POMELO, SHADDOCK)

(Citrus maxima)

TROPICAL

Ancestor of the grapefruit and one of the largest citrus fruits; it ranges from large grapefruit to melon size.

Very thick, coarse yellow to pink skin. Like the grapefruit, the segmented flesh varies in color from yellow to pink to red. Variable in acidity and flavor; some varieties are sweet, juicy, and only mildly acidic. Used for juice and in desserts, sorbets or fruit salads, or as a substitute for grapefruit. Native to Southeast Asia and cultivated widely in the tropics as well as the subtropics.

RAMBUTAN

(Nephelium lappaceum)

TROPICAL

Named aptly from Malay word meaning "hair of the head," which refers to the pink, red and/or yellow soft spiny covering of the red shell. It could just as easily have been translated from "hedgehog plugged into a wall socket" if looks are anything to go by.

Sweet, white translucent flesh with a single seed, very similar to the lychee. Mild, refreshing, sub-acid flavor. High in vitamin C. Mostly eaten fresh, or used in fruit salads. The seeds are sometimes roasted. Native to Malaysia and Southeast Asia. Available mid-summer through early winter.

SAPODILLA
(NISPERO)

(Manilkara zapota)

TROPICAL

Tree is the source of *chicle*—a white sap valued by pre-Columbian Indians—originally used in chewing gum.

Round to oval in shape with potato-like russet brown, thin, rough-textured skin. Soft, slightly grainy flesh; yellowish (to yellowish-brown) aromatic flesh when ripe. The flavor is meltingly honey sweet and caramel-like or maple syrupy, but astringent if eaten unripe. Usually eaten fresh when fully ripe or used juiced or in desserts and ice cream. Native to Central America and Mexico and grown throughout the tropics. Available summer through fall.

SOUR ORANGE
(BERGAMOT, BIGARADE, OR SEVILLE)

(Citrus Aurantium)

SUBTROPICAL

Believed to be the ancestor of all oranges. A large orange with a rough, reddish-orange skin. Too astringent to be eaten raw. Juice used in marinades; cooked for sauces and Latin American mojos, and in preserves (e.g., marmalade). The peel is candied, and its oil content used for flavoring foods, liqueurs, and tea. Probably native to China; grown extensively in Spain and the Caribbean.

STAR FRUIT
(CARAMBOLA)

(Averrhoea carambola)

TROPICAL

Named for the unique shape of the fruit in cross-section—which makes it a natural for the food stylists' Hall of Fame. As the fruit ripens and turns golden, the five ribs turn brown.

Thin, waxy skin, with a mild, sweet to sub-acid flesh that is translucent, succulent, soft, and crisp. Some varieties, high in oxalic acid, are puckery-tart; this can be minimized by cutting off the ribs, where most of the acid is concentrated. The flavor combines apple, grape, and citrus tones. Mostly eaten fresh or in fruit salads and as garnish. Best chilled; also juiced. Less ripe fruit is best pickled and used in preserves and chutneys. Native to Java and Southeast Asia, now grown extensively in Taiwan, Malaysia, the Caribbean, Hawaii, and Florida. Available mid-summer to mid-winter.

SUGAR APPLE
(SWEETSOP)

(Annona Squamosa)

TROPICAL

Related to the cherimoya and guanabana. Variety pictured is the extraordinary Kampong Mauve; other varieties have a yellow-green or red skin. The heart-shaped fruit's skin bursts open as it ripens. The delicious, sweet white or yellow creamy flesh is divided into segments, somewhat like citrus fruit, and contains several shiny seeds. Eaten fresh, in fruit salads, and used in desserts, ice cream, and drinks. Native to the tropics of the Americas. Also grown in Florida and California. Available mid-summer through mid-winter.

TAMARILLO
(TREE TOMATO)

(Cyphomandra betacea)

SUBTROPICAL

Related to the tomato and eggplant. The "cross-dresser" of the fruit world: with a little sugar, it is a dessert; with vinegar and pepper, it is savory.

Oval or egg-shaped fruit, like a plum tomato. Golden yellow or scarlet skin and flesh, with purple seeds. The glossy, bitter skin is best peeled off by blanching. Strong bittersweet (though pleasant) flavor, not unlike that of the tomato; the yellow variety is a little sweeter. Eaten fresh, in salads, stewed, and chilled. Also used in sauces, drinks, or for relishes and preserves. Native to the South American Andes. Also grown in the Caribbean, New Zealand, Australia, and Asia. Available late spring through fall.

TAMARIND
(TAMARINDO)

(Tamarindus indica)

TROPICAL

The tamarind is a large, spreading semi-evergreen tropical legume. Long, brown bean-like brittle pods contain up to twelve seeds and sticky brown tart-sweet pulp. The pulp has a flavor akin to dates mixed with lemon and peaches. Soaked, strained pulp used as a flavoring in drinks, sauces (including Worcestershire sauce), grilling glazes, curries, preserves, and chutney. Available in pulp and paste form. Native to India. Also grown extensively in Africa, Southeast Asia and Mexico.

UNIQUE FRUIT
(UNIQ FRUIT OR UGLI TANGELO)

(Citrus, spp.)

SUBTROPICAL

A hybrid of the grapefruit, tangerine, and sour orange. Rather lumpy-looking with very thick greenish-orange skin that fits rather loosely over the fruit sections. Fragrant, juicy, orange-yellow flesh has a sweet-acid flavor somewhere between orange and grapefruit. Few seeds, high in vitamin C. Eaten fresh and used much like grapefruit. Native to Jamaica. Available winter through spring.

VELVET APPLE
(MABOLO)

(Diospyros discolor)

TROPICAL

Related to the hardwood ebony tree and the persimmon. Oval or rounded fruit is sometimes a little flat in shape. The skin is pink, brown, or purple in color and covered with furry-soft, reddish-brown velvety hair. Sweet, creamy flesh has a sub-acid flavor and an aroma that is sometimes cheeselike. Eaten fresh and used in desserts. Native to the Philippines. Available mostly in the fall.

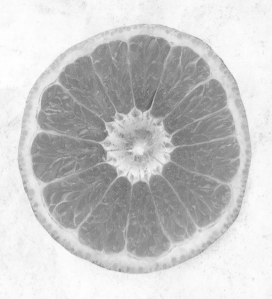

WAMPI

(Clausena lansium)

TROPICAL

The grape-like, pale yellow fruit grows in clusters
from ornamental trees. The aromatic, soft flesh has
a jelly-like consistency and a sweet, sub-acid flavor.
High in vitamin C. Eaten ripe and used in desserts,
curries, and preserves. Native to South China.

WAX JAMBU
(JAVA APPLE)

(Syzygium samarangense)

TROPICAL

This round to pear-shaped fruit grows in clusters
on fast-growing evergreen trees. It looks like candy
and has a crunchy texture. The crisp, juicy flesh
tastes faintly sweet. The redder the flesh, the
sweeter its flavor. Mostly eaten fresh. Native to
Southeast Asia.

WHITE SAPOTE
(MATASANO)

(Casimiroa edulis)

SUBTROPICAL

The fruit's bright green skin turns light yellow
when ripe. Greenish-yellow to cream-yellow flesh
when ripe. Delicate, sweet flavor with a smooth,
creamy consistency. Tones of avocado.

Mostly eaten fresh, used for fruit salads,
sauces, desserts, milk shakes, and preserves. Native
to Mexico and Central America. Available May
through August.

COUNTER CLOCKWISE FROM TOP: *Shocking Pink Limeade;*
Pineapple and Sugarcane Moonshine Chutney; Homemade Key
Lime Mustard; Ancho Chile and Guava Glazed Smoked
Ham Sandwich

Beverages

SHOCKING PINK LIMEADE

Key limes are interchangeable with Mexican limes, but you can use the larger, thicker-skinned Persian limes if necessary. You can prepare the limeade concentrate well beforehand and keep in the refrigerator until needed.

1 cup prickly pear juice, strained

$\frac{1}{2}$ cup fresh Key lime juice

$\frac{1}{2}$ cup sugar

2 cups sparkling water

Shaved ice, or ice cubes

**6 lime wedges,
    for garnish**

Place the prickly pear juice, lime juice, and sugar in a jar with a tight-fitting lid, and shake vigorously to dissolve the sugar. Alternatively, mix all the ingredients together in a blender.

Pour $\frac{1}{4}$ cup of the liquid into a tall, chilled glass and add $\frac{1}{3}$ cup of the sparkling water. Stir well, fill each glass with shaved ice or ice cubes, and garnish with a lime wedge.

Yield: 6 servings

PUCKERY PRICKLY PEAR LIMEADE

This is simply a refreshing, alcoholic version of the previous limeade recipe. Add more or less vodka, to taste.

1 cup prickly pear juice, strained

$\frac{1}{2}$ cup fresh Key lime juice

$\frac{1}{2}$ cup sugar

1$\frac{1}{8}$ cups citron flavored vodka

2 cups sparkling water

Shaved ice, or ice cubes

6 lime wedges, for garnish

Place the prickly pear juice, lime juice, and sugar in a jar with a tight-fitting lid, and shake vigorously to dissolve the sugar. Alternatively, mix all the ingredients together in a blender.

Pour $\frac{1}{4}$ cup of the liquid into a glass. Add 1 jigger (1$\frac{1}{2}$ ounces or 3 tablespoons) of the vodka and $\frac{1}{3}$ cup of the sparkling water. Stir well, fill each glass with shaved ice or ice cubes, and garnish with a lime wedge.

Yield: 6 servings

BATIDO EXÓTICO

Exotic (or *exótico* in Spanish) is how most batidos (or fruit drinks or shakes) may seem at first to many North Americans, but in South America and many places in the Caribbean, they are as common as milk shakes. It is nice to know that you're getting a lot of wonderful fruit into the bargain.

> 1 cup peeled, seeded, and roughly chopped papaya
>
> 1 cup peeled, pitted, and roughly chopped mango
>
> 2 cups peeled, cored, and roughly chopped pineapple
>
> 2 small, ripe bananas, peeled, and roughly chopped
>
> 3 tablespoons fresh lime juice
>
> 1 $\frac{1}{2}$ cups coconut milk
>
> 2 tablespoons sugar
>
> 8 ice cubes

Place the papaya, mango, pineapple, bananas, and lime juice in a blender, and blend until smooth. Add the coconut milk, sugar and some ice cubes and blend again until the ice is smooth.

Pour into tall, chilled glasses. Garnish with tropical fruits of your choice.

Yield: 4 to 6 servings

BAHAMA MAMA MAMEY MILK SHAKE

The mamey sapote should be chilled before using in this recipe. Add half a ripe banana for even more tropical flavor.

4 cups peeled and pitted mamey sapote

1½ cups milk

1 cup chilled coconut milk

¾ cup vanilla ice cream

6 to 8 ice cubes

Place all the ingredients in a blender and blend until smooth.

Pour into tall, chilled glasses and serve.

Yield: 4 servings

TAMARIND TWISTER

The tamarind, sugar, and water "base" for this drink served over ice also makes a very nice, cooling beverage. Note that the Preserve of Six Citrus Fruits needs to steep overnight.

> **2 cups Preserve of Six Citrus Fruits with Five Spice Powder (recipe follows)**
>
> **I cup tamarind pulp**
>
> **½ cup sugar**
>
> **6 cups water**
>
> **Ice cubes, cracked**

Prepare the Six Citrus Preserves with Five Spice Powder.

Place the tamarind and sugar together in a non-reactive bowl and set aside. In a saucepan, bring the water to almost boiling and pour over the tamarind and sugar. Stir together and allow the mixture to steep for 15 minutes, stirring and mashing a couple of times. Strain the mixture and chill in the refrigerator.

For each cocktail, mix ¾ cup of the chilled tamarind mixture with ⅓ cup of the Six Citrus Fruits Preserves with Five Spice Powder (both liquid and a little of the fruit). Pour over cracked ice and serve.

Yield: 6 servings

PRESERVE OF SIX CITRUS FRUITS WITH FIVE SPICE POWDER

If the kumquat or calomondin are unavailable, use another orange or blood orange.

- **1 lime**
- **1 orange**
- **1 lemon**
- **1 kumquat**
- **1 calomondin**
- **1 small grapefruit**
- **1 tablespoon Chinese five spice powder**
- **2 cups sugar**
- **2 cups water**
- **Zest of 3 limes (about 1 tablespoon)**

Cut the lime, orange, lemon, kumquat, calomondin, and grapefruit into round slices ⅓-inch thick; discard the ends. Then cut each lime, orange, and lemon slice into 4 quarters, the kumquat and calomondin slices in half, and the grapefruit slices into eighths. Place all the fruit in a mixing bowl, add the five spice powder, toss together and set aside.

Place the sugar, water, and lime zest in a non-reactive saucepan and boil gently for 15 minutes. Strain, and let cool slightly. Pour the liquid over the fruit and let the mixture steep overnight, covered in the refrigerator.

The next day, strain the syrup into a heavy saucepan; reserve the fruit. Reduce the syrup over medium-high heat to 2 cups, about 35 to 40 minutes. Let cool and then pour over the fruit again. Cover and store in the refrigerator until needed.

Yield: About 1 quart

A SUN-BURNED RUM RUNNER

Rum-runners were notorious during the Prohibition era for making the crossing between Cuba and Cayo Hueso (Key West) and keeping spirits afloat (in more than one sense!). It is worth making the homemade grenadine syrup if you have time, as the commercial variety is made with artificial additives. It will keep for months in the refrigerator, tightly covered.

FOR THE GRENADINE:

4 large pomegranates

2 cups sugar

FOR THE DRINK:

3 tablespoons (2 jiggers) white rum

½ tablespoon fresh lime juice

2 tablespoons fresh grapefruit juice

Crushed ice

To remove the seeds from the pomegranate, cut off the bloom end and score the pomegranate from top to bottom. Break the sections over a bowl and remove the seeds with your fingers. Pull away any bitter white membrane and discard together with the peel.

Place 2 cups of the seeds in a bowl with the sugar, and mash them together for a few minutes. Cover and let stand overnight. Reserve the remaining seeds in a glass container, covered and refrigerated.

Transfer the seed and sugar mixture into a small heavy saucepan. Bring to a boil and simmer for 2 minutes, while stirring. Strain through a colander into a clean bowl, pressing down on the seeds to extract as much juice as possible. Discard the seeds and reserve this syrupy mixture in a sterilized glass container.

Press the remaining (uncooked) seeds through the colander into a small heavy saucepan; discard the seeds. Reduce the juice over medium-high heat until only 2 tablespoons remain. Add to the reserved syrup, stir together, and keep until needed. (The reduced juice gives the grenadine a more intense fruit flavor than the commercial grenadine, and avoids food coloring.)

To make the drink, place $\frac{1}{2}$ tablespoon of the grenadine with the rum, lime juice, grapefruit juice, and a scoop of ice in a cocktail shaker. Shake vigorously and strain into a cold champagne flute.

Yield: I serving

SAPODILLA ROOT BEER FLOAT
(A.K.A. THE TROPICAL BLACK COW)

Garnishes such as whipped cream and diced fresh fruit are appropriate embellishments, but this classic is memorable just as it is, with its twist of tropicality.

⅔ cups sugar

1 vanilla bean

2 cups heavy cream

4 extra large egg yolks

1 cup strained sapodilla purée

4 to 6 cups chilled root beer

Sprinkle a little of the sugar on a cutting board. Split the vanilla bean in half lengthwise, and scrape the seeds out onto the sugar. Smear the seeds around and into the sugar (this will separate the seeds and produce flecks in the sugar).

In a saucepan, combine the cream with half of the vanilla-sugar mixture and the vanilla bean pod. Bring to only just boiling over medium heat, stirring occasionally. Meanwhile, combine the egg yolks and the remaining sugar in a mixing bowl. Temper the yolk mixture by slowly whisking in some of the hot cream. Return to the saucepan and continue to cook over low heat, stirring constantly with a wooden spoon for about 1 minute, or until the mixture coats the back of the spoon.

Transfer the mixture to the refrigerator or chill in a stainless steel bowl set over ice, stirring occasionally. Remove the vanilla bean. Whisk in the sapodilla purée—add more or less to taste, as the ripeness of the fruit will determine the intensity of the flavor. Place in an ice cream machine and freeze according to the manufacturer's instructions. Reserve in the freezer, covered.

To make the float, put 1 to 2 large scoops of the prepared sapodilla ice cream into 4 tall, chilled glasses. Pour the cold root beer over the ice cream and serve.

Yield: 4 servings

Soups, Starters, & Salads

CHILLED EXOTIC FRUIT SOUP

Substitute fruits you prefer or varieties that are in season and look good at the market.

FOR THE SOUP:

2 cups water

¼ cup honey

½ Scotch bonnet chile, seeded

½ tablespoon minced ginger

I vanilla bean, split in half lengthwise

Zest of ½ lime

Zest of ½ orange

I stalk lemon grass, trimmed and roughly chopped

2 tablespoons chopped mint leaves

I star anise

FOR THE FRUIT:

¼ cup peeled, pitted, and diced mango

¼ cup peeled, cored, and diced pineapple

¼ cup peeled, sectioned, and sliced blood orange

¼ cup peeled, seeded, and diced mamey sapote

¼ cup peeled, seeded, and diced Charantais melon

4 lychees, peeled

6 jaboticabas, sliced in half

¼ cup coconut meat, thinly sliced, toasted, and broken into bite-size pieces

2 passion fruit, cut in half crosswise

2 finger bananas, peeled and sliced in half lengthwise

I star fruit, cut into slices ¼-inch thick

Place all of the soup ingredients in a saucepan and bring to a simmer. Turn off the heat and let steep for 30 minutes. Strain through a fine mesh strainer into a bowl and chill the liquid thoroughly; discard the solids.

Divide the mango, pineapple, orange, mamey sapote, melon, lychees, and jaboticaba between 4 chilled soup bowls. Pour the soup over the fruit.

Garnish with the coconut, passion fruit halves (cut side up), banana, and star fruit.

Yield: 4 servings

DOUBLE FRUIT COCKTAIL "STRAIGHT UP"

This appetizer is simply freshly juiced pineapple infused with some spices, and then strained to flavor fresh fruit. The flavors are lighter and more natural than typical fruit cocktail syrups. It is called a double fruit cocktail because this way, you get a double intensity of fruit flavor from the syrup.

FOR THE JUICE SYRUP INFUSION:

2 cups fresh pineapple juice

I stick cinnamon or canela

6 allspice berries

I star anise

FOR THE FRUIT COCKTAIL:

$\frac{1}{2}$ cup peeled, cored, and diced pineapple

$\frac{1}{2}$ cup peeled, pitted, and diced mango

$\frac{1}{2}$ cup peeled, seeded, and diced papaya

$\frac{1}{2}$ cup peeled, seeded, and diced cherimoya

I banana, peeled and diced

I Asian pear, peeled, seeded, and diced

I cup mixed fresh fruit (sugar apple, canistel, white sapote, mamey sapote, or sapodilla, or colorful berries)

To prepare the infusion, heat the pineapple juice in a small, heavy saucepan with the spices over medium heat. Reduce the liquid to 1 cup, about 20 minutes, skimming off any foam as necessary. Strain the liquid into a bowl and chill thoroughly.

Combine all the fruit in a mixing bowl, tossing gently. Pour the chilled infusion over the fruit and stir gently. Chill for at least 1 hour, covered. Scoop into chilled fruit cocktail glasses and serve. Garnish with a dollop of yogurt or mint sprigs, or fruit wedges, as desired.

Yield: About 4 cups

JAMAICAN RED BANANA AND PEANUT FRITTERS

WITH AN ORANGE MARMALADE, HORSERADISH, AND SCOTCH BONNET JAM

You can use regular bananas instead of the red. I use 2 spoons for the batter; one to measure and the other to push the mixture into the pan.

FOR THE JAM:

- 6 tablespoons orange marmalade
- $\frac{1}{4}$ cup prepared horseradish
- 2 Scotch bonnet or habanero chiles, seeded and minced
- 4 cloves garlic, minced
- 6 tablespoons honey
- 2 tablespoons Spanish sherry vinegar
- Salt and freshly cracked black pepper, to taste

FOR THE FRITTERS:

- 1¼ cups all-purpose flour, sifted
- 2½ tablespoons baking powder
- 2 tablespoons sugar
- 1 tablespoon chile molido or pure red chile powder
- ½ teaspoon salt
- 3 or 4 red bananas, peeled and roughly chopped (about 1¾ cups)
- ½ cup unsalted Spanish peanuts, toasted and roughly chopped
- 3 extra large eggs, beaten
- ¾ cup milk
- Peanut or canola oil for deep frying

Combine all of the jam ingredients in a mixing bowl and set aside (the yield will be about 1¼ cups).

To prepare the fritters, mix the flour, baking powder, sugar, chile molido, and salt together in a bowl. Mash the bananas and peanuts together in a separate bowl. In a third bowl, whisk the eggs and milk together and then stir into the flour mixture. Add the banana-peanut mixture and thoroughly combine.

Preheat the oil in a deep fryer to 360 degrees. Take 1 tablespoon of the batter, drop into the hot oil, and fry for 1 minute. Fry in batches and drain on paper towels. Keep warm, and serve with the jam as a dipping sauce.

Yield: 8 to 10 appetizers

CHERIMOYA-AVOCADO SALAD
WITH CRISPY CHINESE CHICKEN, ROASTED CASHEW NUTS, AND A PASSION FRUIT DRESSING

This recipe makes four big starters or light dinners, depending on the size of your appetites! A nice touch is to garnish the top of the salad with a wedge of cherimoya (skin on and seed in) to show your guests how attractive the fruit is in its whole form. For an even more colorful presentation, you can serve the cherimoya-avocado salad in a nest of radicchio.

MARINADE:

3 tablespoons light soy sauce

1 teaspoon Chinese five spice powder

2 cloves minced garlic

1 Scotch bonnet or habanero chile, seeded and minced

3 tablespoons honey

1 tablespoon dark roasted sesame oil

Freshly toasted and cracked black pepper to taste

4 boneless chicken breasts, about 8 ounces each, skin on

DRESSING:

$\frac{1}{2}$ cup strained fresh passion fruit juice

$\frac{1}{2}$ cup canola oil

2 teaspoons honey

2 teaspoons light soy sauce

Salt and freshly cracked black pepper, to taste

SALAD:

1 ripe cherimoya, peeled, seeded, and diced

1 Haas or $\frac{1}{2}$ Florida ripe avocado, peeled, pitted, and diced

$\frac{1}{2}$ cup unsalted cashew nuts, roasted until crisp (optional)

Combine the marinade ingredients in a large mixing bowl. Add the chicken and marinate, covered, in the refrigerator for at least 1 hour, and up to 8 hours. Turn the chicken over at least once.

Combine all the dressing ingredients and keep covered in the refrigerator.

Place the avocado and cherimoya in a mixing bowl and toss with $\frac{1}{4}$ cup of the dressing. Keep refrigerated until ready to serve.

Prepare the grill or broiler. When hot, cook the chicken breasts, turning as needed until cooked through. Transfer to a warm platter (you may discard the skin at this stage if you wish).

Mound the cherimoya-avocado salad at the top of each serving plate. Spoon the dressing onto the plates as a dipping sauce for the chicken. Cut the chicken into thin slices and place next to the salad, garnishing with the cashews.

Yield: 4 servings

MIXED GREENS AND FRUITS SALAD
WITH TOASTED PISTACHIOS AND WARM LOXAHATCHEE CHEVRE

Turtle Creek Farms in Loxahatchee, Florida makes some wonderful goat cheeses, including the chevre I use here. There are a growing number of excellent family-scale artisan cheese makers around the country who do not have big advertising budgets. I urge you to support them—the small growers and farmers are still what makes America strong. By all means substitute a Maytag blue or a mozzarella (preferably from the Dallas Mozzarella Company) if you prefer.

FOR THE FRUITS:

- **2 figs, stemmed and quartered**
- **I star fruit (carambola), thinly sliced**
- **I kiwi fruit, peeled, halved, and thinly sliced crosswise**
- **I sapodilla, peeled, cored, and sliced into thin wedges (optional)**
- **½ cup peeled and diced mango**
- **I ruby grapefruit or pummelo, peeled and sectioned**
- **½ cup peeled, cored, and diced pineapple**

FOR THE SALAD:

- **6 tablespoons extra-virgin olive oil**

- **2 tablespoons balsamic vinegar**

- **Salt and freshly ground black pepper, to taste**

- **2 double handfuls of washed mixed lettuces such as romaine, red leaf, radicchio, bibb, and endive**

- **½ cup toasted pistachio nuts**

- **4 slices (½ inch thick by 6 inches wide) wheat, sourdough, or country-style bread**

- **4 ounces soft fresh goat cheese at room temperature**

In a mixing bowl, gently mix all the fruit together and keep covered in the refrigerator until ready to serve.

In a separate bowl, mix together the oil, vinegar, salt, and pepper. Rip the lettuces, add to the bowl with the nuts, and toss thoroughly. Adjust the seasoning and place in the middle of four large serving bowls. Arrange the fruits over the lettuce. Toast the slices of bread, spread evenly with the goat cheese, and serve on the side of each plate.

Yield: 4 servings

FROM TOP: *Key West Sweet Plantain Stuffed and Spiced Pork Tenderloin with a Sour Orange Marinade; Pomegranate Molasses Marinated and Grilled Lamb Chops with Pomegranate-Lamb Jus*

Main Dishes

KEY WEST SWEET PLANTAIN STUFFED AND SPICED PORK TENDERLOIN
WITH A SOUR ORANGE MARINADE

If sour oranges are unavailable, substitute an extra orange and an extra lime in the marinade. You can make this dish without the plantain stuffing, if you prefer. In Key West, this dish is traditionally served with slices of raw red onion, but you can serve it with side dishes of your choice.

FOR THE MARINADE:

- $\frac{1}{2}$ red onion, peeled and thinly sliced
- I head garlic, cut in half crosswise and broken up (root discarded)
- I sour orange, cut in half
- I orange, cut in half
- I lime, cut in half
- I Scotch bonnet or habanero chile, cut in half (optional)
- 12 black peppercorns, toasted and slightly crushed
- I bay leaf, broken
- $\frac{1}{2}$ bunch cilantro, roughly chopped (optional)
- I cup virgin olive oil
- 2 pork tenderloins, about 10 ounces each, completely trimmed

STUFFING:

- 2 tablespoons peanut or canola oil
- 2 very ripe plantains, peeled and cut into slices $\frac{1}{2}$-inch thick
- 4 tablespoons butter, cut into small pieces
- Salt and freshly ground black pepper, to taste
- 2 teaspoons toasted and ground cumin
- 2 teaspoons toasted and ground black peppercorns
- I teaspoon sugar
- I teaspoon salt
- 2 tablespoons peanut oil

Combine all the marinade ingredients in a non-reactive bowl; squeeze the fruit and add it to the marinade as well as the juice. Cut the pork tenderloins in half crosswise, to yield 4 portions, and place in the marinade. Keep refrigerated for at least 2 hours and up to 8 hours, turning occasionally.

To prepare the stuffing, heat the oil in a sauté pan or skillet. Sauté the plantain slices until dark on both sides. Drain on paper towels and let cool. Transfer to a bowl and mash with the butter. Season with salt and pepper and set aside.

Preheat the oven to 400 degrees. Remove the pork from the marinade and pat dry (you can freeze the marinade and use one more time if you like). Make a narrow, deep slit in the side of each piece of pork to form a pocket; do not cut all the way through and only to $\frac{1}{2}$ inch from each end. Pack the plantain stuffing in the center of each tenderloin portion and press the meat together to close the stuffed pocket.

Combine the cumin, pepper, sugar, and salt in a bowl and sprinkle over the meat, gently rubbing it in. Tie the pork with butcher's twine in 2 or 3 places to secure.

Heat the oil in a cast-iron skillet or ovenproof sauté pan and sear the pork on all sides for 2 minutes over medium-high heat. Drain any excess oil from the skillet and place the skillet in the oven for 7 or 8 minutes.

Remove the pork and let the portions rest for a few minutes. Cut the twine and slice the meat. Arrange in a fan on serving plates and serve.

Yield: 4 servings

FISH AND FRUIT "PORT OF CALL"

"Port of Call" was the finest restaurant in Key West in its time. I adapted this dish, famous in the Florida Keys, and in turn, it became much requested in my restaurants. The fish is smothered with sweet tropical fruits, *étouffée*-style, which makes it a great way to get children to eat fish. The almonds I added as a final twist give the dish a nice crunch.

FOR THE FRUIT AND GARNISH:

- **1 cup sliced almonds**
- **Salt and freshly ground black pepper, to taste**
- **1⅓ tablespoons red currant jelly**
- **1 teaspoon ground cinnamon**
- **1½ tablespoons butter, cut into small pieces**
- **1 cup peeled, pitted, and diced mango**
- **¾ cup peeled, seeded, and diced papaya**
- **1 banana, peeled and diced**
- **1 ripe tomato, peeled, seeded, and diced**

FOR THE FISH:

- **1 extra large egg**
- **¼ cup half and half**
- **Salt and freshly ground black pepper, to taste**
- **4 yellowtail snapper fillets (or regular snapper, or other delicate fish), boneless and skinless, about 8 ounces each**
- **¼ cup all-purpose flour**
- **¼ cup clarified butter**

Place the almonds in a small, dry skillet over medium heat. Toss occasionally until they turn golden brown. Season with salt and pepper and set aside.

In a saucepan, heat the jelly and cinnamon over low heat until just melted. Add the butter and let it melt. Add the mango, papaya, banana, and tomato; heat through. Keep warm.

Preheat the oven to 425 degrees. In a large

mixing bowl, beat the egg with the half and half, salt and pepper. Dredge the fillets in the flour, shaking off any excess and let sit in the egg wash.

Heat the clarified butter in a large cast-iron skillet or ovenproof sauté pan over medium-high heat. Remove the fish from the egg wash and carefully lay it in the pan, making sure it falls away from you to avoid spattering butter. Gently shake the pan and cook for 2 to 3 minutes or until a deep golden color. Carefully turn over with a spatula or tongs. Cook briefly to brown the other side, and then drain off the excess butter from the pan. Transfer the skillet to the oven and cook for 7 to 10 minutes, depending on the thickness of the fish.

Place the fish on warm serving plates. Ladle the warm sauce over the fish and sprinkle the almonds on top. Serve with the side dishes of your choice.

Yield: 4 servings

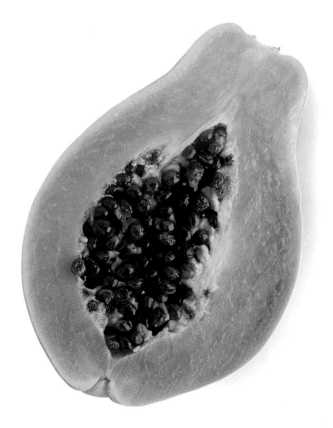

POMEGRANATE MOLASSES MARINATED AND GRILLED LAMB CHOPS WITH A POMEGRANATE-LAMB JUS

The Middle Eastern and North African heritage of the Spanish conquerors is evident in so many of the flavors that have become part of the New World Cuisine—the amalgam of Central and South American, Caribbean, and Floridian cooking. This slightly sweet marinade and the robust, gamey flavor of the lamb go perfectly with the Pummelo Juice Couscous (page 125). Some simply sautéed eggplant further conjures up images of Moroccan *soukhs,* bright *djellabas,* and parading peacocks that are part of the scenery while traveling by train into Marrakesh. Pomegranate molasses are a Lebanese specialty, available in Middle Eastern, some Italian, and specialty grocery stores.

FOR THE LAMB AND MARINADE:

8 lamb rib chops, trimmed, about 4 ounces each

Salt and freshly ground black pepper, to taste

1 tablespoon rosemary leaves

¼ cup pomegranate molasses

4 cloves garlic, thinly sliced

2 bay leaves, broken

⅓ cup virgin olive oil

FOR THE JUS:

1 tablespoon butter

1 tablespoon virgin olive oil

4 shallots, minced

4 cloves garlic, minced

1 cup fresh pomegranate juice

2 tablespoons red wine vinegar

3 cups lamb or chicken stock

Rub the lamb chops with the salt, pepper, and rosemary leaves. Combine the molasses, garlic, bay leaves, and oil in a non-reactive bowl and add the lamb chops, turning over a few times to coat thoroughly. Cover and refrigerate up to 4 hours before cooking.

To prepare the jus, heat $\frac{1}{2}$ tablespoon of the butter and all the oil in a saucepan. When the butter melts, add the shallots and garlic and sauté over medium heat for about 3 minutes, or until lightly colored; stir frequently. Add the pomegranate juice and vinegar and reduce the liquid by half. Add the stock and reduce for about 15 minutes, skimming as necessary, or until the sauce coats the back of a spoon.

Remove the pan from the heat and strain through a fine mesh strainer into a clean saucepan. Keep warm.

Prepare the grill, or heat a grill pan. Remove the lamb chops from the marinade and season with salt and pepper. Grill for 4 minutes per side for rare, or 5 to 6 minutes for medium-rare.

Bring the sauce to just under a boil and whisk in the remaining $\frac{1}{2}$ tablespoon of butter. Divide the sauce between 4 warm serving plates and place the lamb chops on top. Serve with the sides of your choice. Garnish with fresh pomegranate seeds, if desired.

Yield: 4 servings

ANCHO CHILE AND GUAVA GLAZED SMOKED HAM

This main course recipe also makes for some memorable leftover ham sandwiches with a dollop of Homemade Key Lime Mustard (page 119). These are best made with traditional rye bread or toasted Cuban bread, with pickles, tomatoes, romaine lettuce, and such. The glaze will cover 1 whole ham, or it can be used on half of a ham with the other half of the glaze lasting in the refrigerator for up to 6 months or more. The Pineapple-Scotch Bonnet Mojo (page 113) goes nicely with this ham recipe too.

GLAZE:

4 ancho chiles, seeded

12 cloves garlic

1½ quarts water

1¼ cup guava jam

3 tablespoons Spanish sherry vinegar

½ teaspoon salt

1 tablespoon freshly cracked black pepper

1 smoked ham (butt portion)

Toast the chiles in a dry skillet over medium heat for 1 or 2 minutes or until fragrant; take care not to let them burn or they may taste bitter. Chop roughly and transfer to a saucepan together with the garlic and water. Bring to a medium-high boil over high heat. Reduce the liquid until it has almost all evaporated, about 50 to 60 minutes. Remove the pan from the heat and set aside.

Place the guava jam in a saucepan and warm over medium heat until melted. Set aside.

Transfer the cooked chile and garlic mixture to a food processor or blender and pulse. Add the melted jam, vinegar, salt, and pepper, and process until blended. Reserve the glaze until needed (the yield will be about 1¾ cups).

Cook the ham as you normally would; you can grill it or bake in an oven preheated to 325 to 350 degrees, on a roasting rack set in a roasting pan. After 1 hour, baste with the glaze. Then baste every 15 to 20 minutes, until cooked through (this will take a total of 2 to 2½ hours).

Let the ham rest for 10 to 15 minutes. Cut into slices and serve, making sure each helping has some of the dark, caramelized edges. Serve with the side dishes of your choice.

Yield: 10 to 12 servings (plus leftovers!)

FROM TOP TO BOTTOM: *Deep Dish Asian Pear Pie; Creamy, But Frozen Passion; Rum Caramel-Espresso Poached 'Niño' Banana Splits; Candied Kumquat Key Lime Pie*

Salsas, Chutneys, Condiments, & Preserves

ALL-PURPOSE EXOTIC FRUIT SALSA

All-purpose for savory dishes, that is (for a dessert salsa see the Fruit Salsa Sweet Speckled Pizza Pie, on page 134). Salsa and grilled foods (in particular) are a partnership that has stood the test of taste and time. The variations are endless. *The Great Salsa Book,* written by my friend Mark Miller, will take you on a first-rate voyage into the fiery, libidinous and fun loving heart of salsa!

- ½ **cup fresh orange juice**
- **1 cup peeled and seeded papaya, diced small**
- **1 cup peeled and cored pineapple, diced small**
- **1 or 2 Scotch bonnet chiles, seeded and minced**
- **1 jalapeño chile, seeded and minced**
- ¼ **cup red onion, diced small**
- **3 tablespoons olive oil**
- **Salt and freshly ground black pepper, to taste**

In a saucepan, reduce the orange juice over medium-high heat to about 2 tablespoons. Remove from the heat and allow to cool slightly. Place the remaining ingredients in a mixing bowl and thoroughly combine with the reduced orange juice.

Yield: About 2½ cups

BAJAN AVOCADO COCKTAIL SALSA

This is my tip of the hat to the flavors of Barbados, whose people are known as *Bajans*. This is a versatile salsa that goes great with tortilla chips; or, you could add some cooked and diced shrimp or shredded crabmeat for a chunky-spicy seafood salsa/salad.

- 1/4 cup ketchup-based chile sauce
- 2 Scotch bonnet or habanero chiles, seeded and minced
- 3 cloves garlic, minced
- 1/2 cup minced red onion
- 1/4 cup roughly chopped cilantro leaves
- 2 tablespoons fresh lime juice
- 1/4 cup prepared horseradish
- 1/4 teaspoon Tabasco™ sauce
- 1/4 teaspoon Worcestershire sauce
- 1 cup peeled, seeded, and diced tomatoes
- 3 scallions, trimmed and finely chopped
- Salt and freshly cracked black pepper, to taste
- 1 cup finely diced ripe avocado

In a mixing bowl, thoroughly combine all the ingredients except for the avocado. Now gently fold in the avocado and adjust the seasoning. Keep chilled; use as soon as possible.

Yield: About 2⅔ cups

EXOTIC FRUITS CURRY

This curry salsa/sauce enlivens simple grilled chicken, assertively flavored fish such as tuna or swordfish, or shellfish dishes, perhaps with a rice pilaf or a firm pasta noodle, like penne.

Tamarind sirop is a sweet fruit syrup made with tamarind pulp, sugar, and water; it is available in Latin American or Caribbean stores.

> **2 tablespoons olive oil**
>
> **2 tablespoons spicy dark roasted sesame oil**
>
> **2 cloves garlic, minced**
>
> **I jalapeño chile, seeded and minced**
>
> **I Scotch bonnet chile, seeded and minced**
>
> **I tablespoon minced ginger**
>
> **I red onion, diced**
>
> **$\frac{1}{2}$ bulb fennel, diced**
>
> **2 tablespoons curry powder**
>
> **I cup fresh orange juice**
>
> **$\frac{1}{2}$ cup tamarind sirop**
>
> **4 ripe red or yellow tamarillos, peeled and diced (seeds left in)**
>
> **I cup heavy cream**
>
> **Salt and freshly ground black pepper, to taste**
>
> **$\frac{1}{2}$ cup peeled, seeded, and diced cherimoya**
>
> **$\frac{1}{2}$ cup peeled, seeded, and diced white sapote**
>
> **$\frac{1}{2}$ cup peeled, pitted, and diced mango**
>
> **I cup peeled, seeded, and diced papaya**

Heat the olive oil and sesame oil together in a large, heavy saucepan. When hot, sauté the garlic, jalapeño, Scotch bonnet chiles, and ginger over medium heat until just fragrant, about $1\frac{1}{2}$ minutes. Add the onion and fennel, turn the heat to high, and sauté for 7 to 8 minutes until caramelized, stirring occasionally.

Add the curry powder, stirring with a wooden spoon for 1 or 2 minutes. Add the orange juice and tamarind sirop, and stir rapidly. Reduce the liquid to 1 cup, about 10 minutes. Strain through a medium mesh strainer into a clean saucepan; discard the vegetables.

Add the tamarillos and bring to a simmer, stirring. Simmer for 10 minutes. Add the cream, turn up the heat, and boil for 2 minutes, stirring. Stir in the diced fruit and just warm through. Season with salt and pepper and reserve until needed. Garnish with more diced fruit, if desired.

Yield: About 2½ cups

PINEAPPLE-SCOTCH BONNET MOJO

Mojos are sauces of Spanish origin that are popular in many parts of Central America and the Caribbean. In Cuba, for example, mojo (pronounced "mo-ho") refers to a specific type of spicy sauce. This recipe makes the perfect condiment for spicy ribs, pork dishes, or grilled chicken.

- ½ **large ripe pineapple, peeled, cored, and roughly chopped**
- ½ **cup fruity California chardonnay wine**
- ¼ **cup fresh orange juice**
- 1 **Scotch bonnet or habanero chile, seeded and minced**

Place the pineapple, chardonnay, and orange juice in a food processor or blender and purée. Transfer to a mixing bowl and stir in the chile. Keep refrigerated for up to 2 days or so. Transfer to a saucepan, stir and warm before serving.

Yield: About 3 cups

PAWPAW PICKLE TARTAR RELISH

The papaya is also known as "pawpaw," especially in the Caribbean, and should not be confused with the North American pawpaw. Use this relish with grilled fish, fish sticks, or as a fish sandwich spread.

FOR THE PICKLED PAWPAW:

- **4 ounces green papaya, peeled and diced**
- **4 cloves garlic, thinly sliced**
- **1 Scotch bonnet or habanero chile, seeded and minced**
- **$\frac{1}{2}$ tablespoon fennel seeds**
- **$\frac{1}{2}$ tablespoon mustard seeds**
- **2 bay leaves**
- **$\frac{1}{2}$ cup apple cider vinegar**
- **$\frac{1}{2}$ cup champagne vinegar**
- **$\frac{1}{2}$ cup water**

FOR THE RELISH:

- **2 extra large egg yolks**
- **2 teaspoons champagne vinegar**
- **5 tablespoons virgin olive oil**
- **6 tablespoons canola oil**
- **2 tablespoons finely diced sweet pickles**
- **$1\frac{1}{2}$ tablespoons finely diced red onion**
- **1 Scotch bonnet or habanero chile, seeded and minced**
- **1 extra large hard-cooked egg**
- **Salt and freshly ground black pepper, to taste**

Combine the papaya, garlic, and chile in a mixing bowl. Place the fennel and mustard seeds in a non-reactive saucepan and toast them over medium heat until they become fragrant. Add the bay leaves, vinegars, and water, and bring to a boil. Remove from the heat and pour over the papaya mixture; keep the solids submerged with a plate and let cool. Reserve at least overnight before using in this recipe. Keep covered in the refrigerator for up to 1 month or bottle.

Mince 3 tablespoons of the pickled papaya and set aside. Whisk the egg yolks in a blender, or by hand, until pale. Whisk in the vinegar and then the olive oil and canola oil gradually until it is all incorporated. Transfer to a bowl (if using a blender) and gently stir in the reserved minced pickled papaya, 1½ tablespoons of the pickling juice, pickles, onion and chile. Sieve the cooked egg yolk into the mixture, and mince the egg white, stirring it in. Season with salt and pepper and keep chilled until ready to use. Use within 2 or 3 days.

Yield: About 1⅓ cups

SWEET AND SOUR JABOTICABAS WITH FIRE ROASTED PEARL ONIONS

This recipe is an adaptable partner for braised dishes, especially duck or chicken legs.

> **24 jaboticabas, pierced with the tines of a sharp fork**
>
> **⅓ cup sugar**
>
> **⅓ cup red wine vinegar**
>
> **Zest and juice of 1 orange**
>
> **24 pearl onions, trimmed**
>
> **2 tablespoons virgin olive oil**

Place the jaboticabas, sugar, vinegar, orange zest, and juice in a small saucepan and stir together. Warm over low heat and gently simmer for 5 minutes, stirring once or twice. Strain the liquid into a clean pan and reserve the solids in a mixing bowl. Reduce the liquid over medium heat to ½ cup, about 10 minutes. Pour over the fruit and reserve.

Preheat the oven to 350 degrees. Place the onions in a small ovenproof casserole dish and drizzle with the oil. Roll the onions around a little and roast in the oven until tender, about 45 minutes. Remove and let cool. When the onions are cool enough to handle, pop them out of their skins and add to the jaboticabas. Warm the mixture through and serve.

Yield: 4 to 6 servings

PEPINO, MANGO, AND ASIAN PEAR SLAW

This slaw goes well with a wide variety of dishes, and especially Asian dishes (spring rolls, for example), grilled chicken, tuna, swordfish, or salmon.

DRESSING:

$1\frac{1}{2}$ tablespoons sugar

2 tablespoons fresh lime juice

$\frac{1}{4}$ cup water

2 cloves garlic, minced

1 tablespoon minced cilantro leaves

$\frac{1}{2}$ tablespoon Sriracha hot chile sauce

2 tablespoons Oriental fish sauce

SLAW:

1 pepino (melon pear), peeled, seeded, and cut into 2-inch julienne strips

1 Asian pear, peeled, cored, and cut into 2-inch julienne strips

$\frac{1}{2}$ ripe mango, peeled, pitted, and cut into 2-inch julienne strips

1 carrot, peeled and cut into 2-inch julienne strips

Place the sugar, lime juice, and water in a mixing bowl and stir to dissolve the sugar. Mix in the garlic, cilantro, Sriracha, and fish sauce and set aside.

Mix the pepino, Asian pear, mango, and carrot strips in a separate bowl. Add the liquid mixture, combine, and let stand in the refrigerator for at least 1 hour so the flavors can marry. Drain off the excess liquid and serve.

Yield: About $3\frac{1}{2}$ cups

EAST INDIAN SPICED FRUIT YOGURT

This is a wonderful accompaniment with spicy grilled lamb, among other meat dishes.

- 1 plantain, peeled and cut into slices $\frac{1}{4}$-inch thick
- 1 teaspoon ground cumin
- Salt and freshly cracked black pepper, to taste
- 3 tablespoons butter
- 2 teaspoons black mustard seeds, toasted and lightly crushed
- 2 teaspoons coriander seeds, toasted and lightly crushed
- $\frac{1}{2}$ cup unsweetened dried coconut
- $\frac{1}{2}$ cup peeled and cored pineapple, diced small
- $\frac{1}{2}$ cup peeled and seeded papaya, diced small
- $\frac{1}{2}$ cup peeled and pitted mango, diced small
- $\frac{1}{3}$ cup diced dried Black Mission figs
- $1\frac{1}{2}$ cups plain yogurt

Season the plantain rounds with the cumin, salt and pepper, and set aside.

Heat 1 tablespoon of the butter in a skillet and when hot, add the mustard and coriander seeds. Sauté for 15 seconds over medium-high heat and then stir in the coconut. Allow the coconut to color (about 15 to 20 seconds), and then remove the mixture to a bowl and let cool.

Wipe out the pan and add the remaining 2 tablespoons of butter. Add the seasoned plantain slices and sauté until they are very dark (almost black) on both sides, turning once. Drain on paper towels and when cool, dice small.

Add the plantain, pineapple, papaya, mango, figs, and yogurt to the coconut mixture and gently fold together. Season with salt and pepper and keep refrigerated and covered until needed.

Yield: About 3 cups

HORNED MELON RAITA

The yogurt-based *raitas* of Indian cuisine are wonderfully cooling, especially with hot curries and the like. This particular version also goes very well with lamb in pita bread, or with an eggplant and bell pepper vegetarian combo. For a really impressive presentation, serve this raita in a kiwano half shell.

I kiwano (horned melon), cut in half, flesh scooped out and roughly chopped (about 1/2 cup)

1/4 cup finely chopped red onion

1/2 cup plain yogurt

1/4 cup sour cream

1/2 teaspoon black mustard seeds

1/2 teaspoon cumin seeds

1/4 teaspoon coriander seeds

1/4 teaspoon black peppercorns

1/8 teaspoon garam marsala

1/8 teaspoon chile molido or pure red chile powder

Salt to taste

1/2 tablespoon roughly chopped cilantro leaves

Squeeze the kiwano flesh over a bowl and collect the juice and seeds. Discard the fibrous pulp. Add the onion, yogurt, and sour cream to the kiwano and mix together.

Combine the mustard, cumin and coriander seeds with the peppercorns in a dry skillet. Toast until fragrant and transfer to a spice grinder. Coarsely grind and add to the yogurt mixture. Add the garam marsala, chile powder, salt, and cilantro, and thoroughly combine. Keep covered in the refrigerator until needed.

Yield: About 1 3/4 cups

HOMEMADE KEY LIME MUSTARD

Add a few tablespoons of this mustard to some heavy cream, heat through, and you have a quick and satisfying sauce for grilled chicken or a pepper-crusted strip steak.

$\frac{1}{2}$ cup light mustard seeds

2 tablespoons dry mustard powder

$\frac{1}{2}$ cup water

$\frac{1}{2}$ cup champagne vinegar

3 tablespoons honey

2 tablespoons sugar

$\frac{1}{2}$ tablespoon salt

2 teaspoons toasted and ground coriander seed

I teaspoon finely chopped Key lime zest

I tablespoon Key lime juice

Toast the mustard seeds in a dry skillet until fragrant, and transfer to a spice grinder. Grind to the consistency of fine meal and place in a mixing bowl. Add the mustard powder and water, and mix to a coarse paste. Let stand at room temperature for at least 1 hour for the heat and flavor to develop.

Transfer the mixture to the bowl of a food processor and add the vinegar, honey, sugar, salt, coriander, and lime zest. Process to a smooth paste and then mix in the lime juice. Place in a clean jar and keep refrigerated until needed.

Yield: About I$\frac{1}{2}$ cups

PINEAPPLE AND SUGARCANE MOONSHINE CHUTNEY

This sweet, hot and fruity chutney goes well with grilled pork chops, chicken, or spicy lamb. *Pitú* is a Brazilian sugarcane liquor that smells a little like sweet tequila. Many liquor stores sell *pitú,* but you can use rum or aguardiente equally well. This chutney can be stored for up to a month in an airtight container in the refrigerator.

- 1½ cups peeled, cored, and diced pineapple
- 1¼ cups peeled, pitted, and diced mango
- 1¼ cups peeled, seeded, and diced papaya
- ½ cup diced red onion
- 1 Scotch bonnet or habanero chile, seeded and minced
- ½ tablespoon minced ginger
- ½ cup apple cider vinegar
- ½ cup *pitú*, or white rum
- ½ cup granulated sugar
- ½ cup dark brown sugar
- ¾ teaspoon ground cinnamon
- ½ teaspoon ground allspice

In a mixing bowl, gently combine the pineapple, mango, papaya, onion, chile, and ginger. In a separate bowl, whisk together the vinegar, *pitú,* granulated and brown sugar, cinnamon, and allspice. Pour over the fruit mixture and toss well to combine. Store overnight in the refrigerator.

The next day, transfer the mixture to a large, heavy saucepan and slowly bring to a simmer over medium heat. Reduce the heat to low and simmer gently for 1 hour. Turn off the heat and let cool.

Yield: About 3 cups

Side Dishes

TROPICAL TUBER FRENCH FRIES AND MANGO-TAMARIND KETCHUP

You can blend other flavors (such as mustard) into the ketchup according to personal preference. If you leave the ketchup chunky (rather than puréeing it), you can also use it as a chutney with grilled chicken, for example. Either way, it will last for several weeks in the refrigerator. If yuca is unavailable, use potatoes and proceed as if making regular French fries (you won't need to cook them, like yuca, before frying).

FOR THE KETCHUP:

2 tablespoons canola oil

½ tablespoon ground cumin

I teaspoon ground allspice

I teaspoon ground annatto

I teaspoon crushed dried red pepper

I red onion, diced small

I red bell pepper, seeded and diced small

I Scotch bonnet chile, seeded and minced

I jalapeño chile, seeded and minced

I teaspoon minced garlic

2 ripe mangoes, peeled, pitted, and diced small

½ cup sherry vinegar

I cup fresh pineapple juice

¼ cup tamarind sirop (see note on page 112)

Salt and freshly ground black pepper, to taste

3 tablespoons Pick-a-Peppa sauce

FOR THE FRIES:

**2 pounds yuca, peeled and cut into "planks"
3 inches long**

Vegetable or peanut oil, for frying

**Salt and freshly ground black pepper,
to taste**

To prepare the ketchup, heat the oil in a saucepan over medium-high heat. Add the cumin, allspice, annatto, and dried red pepper. Sauté for 30 seconds, while stirring. Add the onion, bell pepper, chiles, and garlic. Cook for 5 minutes, stirring occasionally.

Add the mangoes, vinegar, pineapple juice, tamarind sirop, salt, and pepper. Bring to a boil, reduce the heat to low and simmer for 20 minutes, stirring occasionally. Add the Pick-a-Peppa sauce and remove from the heat. Allow the mixture to cool. Purée if desired or leave chunky.

For the fries, place the sliced yuca in a large pan and cover with water. Bring to a boil, lower the heat and simmer for 25 to 30 minutes. Drain the yuca, let cool slightly, and cut into ¾-inch wide strips.

Heat the vegetable or peanut oil in a large skillet or deep fryer to 360 degrees. Fry the yuca until golden brown and drain on paper towels. Season to taste with salt and pepper and serve with the ketchup.

Yield: 4 servings

ARROZ CON COCO ORIENTE

You can enhance the Oriental flavors of this rice by adding a few stalks of lemon grass or by adding some minced ginger when cooking the onion.

2 tablespoons dark roasted sesame oil

1 Scotch bonnet or habanero chile, seeded and minced

½ red onion, diced small

1½ tablespoons Thai red curry paste

2 cups short-grain rice

2 cups coconut milk

2 cups chicken stock

Salt and freshly cracked black pepper, to taste

Heat the sesame oil in a large, heavy saucepan. Sauté the chile and onion over medium-high heat for about 3 minutes or until glazed, stirring occasionally.

Add the curry paste and stir well. Add the rice and stir again. Add the coconut milk, stock, salt and pepper, stir well, and bring to a boil. Reduce the heat, cover, and simmer over low heat until the rice is cooked, about 25 minutes. Turn off the heat and let the rice stand for 5 minutes, covered, before serving.

Yield: 8 servings

PUMMELO JUICE COUSCOUS

This side dish goes very well with lamb (see page 104). It can be served hot or cool, and is best presented in a mold. Just lightly oil a ramekin or espresso cup, pack with the cooked couscous, and invert onto serving plates.

2 cups water

I cup couscous

Zest of ½ orange, minced

2 teaspoons toasted and ground cumin seeds

3 tablespoons extra-virgin olive oil

2 tablespoons chopped fresh chives

I tablespoon chopped fresh mint

½ cup fresh pummelo juice, or pink grapefruit juice

Salt and freshly ground black pepper, to taste

Bring the water to a boil and remove from the heat. Stir in the couscous and orange zest. Let stand, covered, for 5 minutes. Add the cumin, oil, chives, mint, and pummelo juice and gently fluff together with a fork so the delicate grains of couscous are not mashed. Season with salt and pepper.

Yield: 4 servings

FROM TOP TO BOTTOM: *Batido Exótico; Jamaican Banana-Pineapple Rum Bread; Mamey Sapote and Cuban Sweet Potato Waffles; Star Fruit Flapjacks*

Brunch, Breads, & Desserts

STAR FRUIT FLAPJACKS

This makes a wonderful breakfast or brunch dish. A host of other fruit can be used instead of the star fruit; just remember that they will need to be enjoyed raw as their brief encounter with the pan will not really cook them. Alternatively, cut fruits can be added to the batter, for a simpler but less visual dish. The batter is best made no more than 1 hour ahead of time.

¾ cup yellow cornmeal

6 tablespoons all-purpose flour

1 tablespoon baking powder

Pinch of salt

2 extra large eggs, separated

1 cup milk

2 tablespoons melted butter

1 tablespoon sugar

Pinch of cream of tartar

3 star fruit, cut into slices ¼-inch thick

Maple syrup, as desired

Combine the cornmeal, flour, baking powder and salt in a mixing bowl. In a separate bowl, beat together the egg yolks, milk, and butter. Add to the dry ingredients and mix together.

In another bowl, whisk the egg whites with the sugar and cream of tartar to medium-stiff peaks. Fold into the corn cake mixture and set the batter aside. Heat a lightly oiled nonstick pan or griddle over medium-high heat. Place one star fruit slice in the pan and ladle 2 tablespoons of the batter squarely over the star fruit. When the batter has plenty of bubbles showing, flip over and cook on the other side for 1 minute. Keep warm while cooking the remaining flapjacks.

Garnish the edges of each serving plate attractively with star fruit slices. Spoon the maple syrup over them and place the flapjacks in the center.

Yield: About 24 cakes (6 servings)

MAMEY SAPOTE AND
CUBAN SWEET POTATO WAFFLES

If Cuban sweet potatoes (also known as *boniato*) are unavailable, use regular sweet potatoes. Sometimes, I dice some very ripe bananas and fold them into the batter.

4 tablespoons butter

1 ½ cups all-purpose flour

1 tablespoon baking powder

1 teaspoon salt

½ teaspoon ground nutmeg

2 tablespoons sugar

½ vanilla bean, split lengthwise and seeds scraped out and reserved

3 extra large eggs, separated

1 cup milk

½ cup cooked and mashed Cuban sweet potatoes

1 ½ cups mamey sapote purée, strained

1 ½ tablespoons safflower (or other light) oil

Melt the butter in a small saucepan and let cool slightly. Meanwhile, sift together the flour, baking powder, salt, and nutmeg in a mixing bowl.

Sprinkle the sugar on a cutting board. Scrape out the vanilla bean seeds onto the sugar and smear around to coat the seeds. Place this mixture in a large mixing bowl and beat with the egg yolks. Add the milk, mashed sweet potato, mamey, oil, melted butter, and dry ingredients, and mix together. Whisk the egg whites to soft peaks in a separate bowl and fold into the mamey–sweet potato mixture.

Cook the batter in a lightly oiled and preheated waffle iron. Serve with the syrup of your choice.

Yield: 8 waffles (4 servings)

JAMAICAN BANANA-PINEAPPLE RUM BREAD

You can use another dried fruit, such as mango or papaya, instead of the pineapple, and you can substitute crème de banana for the rum.

- ½ **cup white rum**
- ½ **cup diced dried pineapple**
- 4 **tablespoons butter**
- ¾ **cup sugar**
- I **extra large egg**
- 2 **very ripe large bananas, mashed**
- ⅓ **cup plain yogurt**
- 2 **cups all-purpose flour**
- ½ **tablespoon baking powder**
- ½ **tablespoon baking soda**
- I **teaspoon ground cinnamon**
- I **teaspoon ground nutmeg**
- I **teaspoon ground allspice**
- ½ **teaspoon salt**
- ½ **cup chopped pecans**

Preheat the oven to 350 degrees.

Place the rum and pineapple in a bowl or measuring cup and let sit, covered, for at least 1 hour.

In the bowl of a mixer (or by hand), beat together the butter and sugar. Add the egg and continue beating until light and fluffy, scraping down the sides of the bowl as necessary. Add the bananas and beat in, mixing well. Beat in the yogurt; do not be alarmed if the mixture looks separated.

In a mixing bowl, combine the flour, baking powder, baking soda, cinnamon, nutmeg, allspice, and salt. Add to the mixer bowl and mix until well blended. Drain the pineapple and fold in with the pecans.

Transfer the batter to a 9-inch loaf pan and bake for 45 to 55 minutes, or until a toothpick comes out clean. Remove the pan from the oven and let it sit for 10 minutes before turning out onto a rack to cool.

Yield: One 9-inch loaf

DEEP DISH ASIAN PEAR PIE

Nothing goes better with this pie than a first-class vanilla ice cream and/or a caramel sauce with a dash of ginger. The filling will seem very wet when you pour it into the crust, but it will firm up as the pie cools.

FOR THE FILLING:

3 pounds Asian pears, peeled and cored

I cup granulated sugar

$\frac{1}{2}$ cup brown sugar

$\frac{1}{2}$ cup apple cider

2 teaspoons ground ginger

$\frac{3}{4}$ teaspoon ground cinnamon

3 tablespoons dried bread crumbs

I prepared pâte brisée-type pie shell

FOR THE TOPPING:

6 tablespoons butter

$\frac{3}{4}$ cup all-purpose flour

$\frac{1}{2}$ cup sugar

$\frac{1}{2}$ cup almond slivers, toasted and roughly chopped

Preheat the oven to 425 degrees. To prepare the filling, slice the pears into $\frac{1}{2}$-inch wedges and place in a large, heavy saucepan. Add the granulated sugar, brown sugar, cider, ginger, and cinnamon. Cook over medium heat until tender, stirring occasionally, about 15 to 20 minutes.

Sprinkle the bread crumbs over the bottom of the pie shell and pour in the Asian pear mixture. Transfer to the oven and bake for 20 minutes.

Meanwhile, to prepare the topping, place the butter, flour, and sugar in a mixing bowl. Cut into the mixture with a pastry cutter until the texture resembles very coarse meal. Stir in the almonds.

Remove the pie from the oven, sprinkle the almond topping evenly over the filling, and return to the oven for 20 minutes longer. Remove from the oven and let cool for at least 1 hour.

Yield: One deep-dish pie

HOT GUANABANA-LIME SOUFFLÉ

Since most people in North America are likely to find fresh guanabana (soursop) difficult to come by, this recipe uses the frozen pulp that is far more readily available. One of the most important aspects of a successful soufflé is consistency, and fresh guanabana is tricky anyway because it is rather gelatinous. The optional lime butter should be poured into the soufflé after you have scooped out and tasted the first bite.

FOR THE SOUFFLÉ:

- 14 ounce package frozen guanabana purée, defrosted
- 1 tablespoon fresh lime juice
- 1 cup heavy cream
- 1/2 cup powdered sugar
- 2 tablespoons all-purpose flour, sifted
- 4 extra large eggs, room temperature, separated
- 2 tablespoons granulated sugar

FOR THE LIME BUTTER (OPTIONAL):

- 4 tablespoons butter, diced
- 1/3 cup sugar
- 1 extra large egg, beaten
- 1/4 cup fresh lime juice
- 1/4 cup heavy cream

Place the guanabana purée in a saucepan and simmer over low heat, stirring, for about 10 minutes or until 1 1/4 cups remain (it should have the consistency of baby food apple sauce). Remove from the heat, stir in the lime juice, and reserve in a cool place.

Preheat the oven to 350 degrees. Lightly butter eight 4-ounce (1/2 cup) soufflé molds or ramekins and dust with a little granulated sugar. Set aside.

In a heavy saucepan, bring the cream to a boil, whisking occasionally. Remove from the heat. Whisk together the powdered sugar and flour in a mixing bowl, and then whisk in the egg yolks until the mixture is thick but not lumpy. Drizzle in some of the hot cream, whisking constantly. Return the mixture to the saucepan with the remaining hot cream and cook over medium heat while whisking until the mixture thickens enough to coat the back of a spoon.

Transfer the mixture to a bowl and add the guanabana and lime mixture. In a separate bowl, whisk the egg whites to soft peaks, taking care not to overwhip. Gradually add the granulated sugar and when incorporated, fold into the guanabana mixture.

Pour into the prepared molds, filling each one to the top. Place in a water bath, making sure the molds do not touch (the water should come about half-way up the side of the molds). Bake on the middle shelf of the oven for about 35 minutes.

If making the lime butter, melt the butter in a double boiler. In a bowl, beat the sugar with the egg and then whisk into the melted butter. Remove the top half of the double boiler and continue to whisk, gradually adding the lime juice and cream. Set aside in a warm place.

Remove the soufflés from the oven. Dust with a little powdered sugar, if desired, and serve immediately with the lime butter.

Yield: 8 servings

FRUIT SALSA SPECKLED SWEET PIZZA PIE WITH A RED TAMARILLO SAUCE

This dessert is an unusual take on a familiar favorite. Make sure the salsa topping is a mixture of ripe, colorful, exotic fruits. Additional garnishes might include chocolate sauce and lightly whipped, sweetened heavy cream.

FOR THE RED TAMARILLO SAUCE:

4 or 5 red tamarillos, peeled

1 tablespoon balsamic vinegar

1 ½ tablespoons sugar

FOR THE FRUIT SALSA TOPPING:

2 cups diced mixed exotic fruits, such as mango, kiwi, papaya, and pomegranate seeds

FOR THE DOUGH:

1 tablespoon dry yeast

¼ cup plus 5 tablespoons warm water (115 to 120 degrees)

½ tablespoon honey

1 ½ cups all-purpose flour

½ teaspoon salt

1 tablespoon extra-virgin olive oil

FOR THE TOPPING:

1 tablespoon warm honey

2 tablespoons chopped mint leaves

6 tablespoons mascarpone or ricotta

In a blender or food processor, purée the tamarillo with the vinegar and sugar, and set aside.

Mix together the fruits for the salsa topping, and keep refrigerated.

To prepare the dough, mix the yeast, ¼ cup of water and honey with a wooden spoon in a mixing bowl. Cover with plastic wrap and set aside for 10 to 15 minutes. Add the flour, salt, oil and remaining water, and knead for 10 minutes. Add a little more flour if necessary.

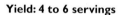

Transfer to a lightly oiled bowl, turning the dough so it is coated with the oil. Cover with plastic wrap and let the dough rise in a warm place for 1½ hours. Punch the dough down, re-cover and let rise for another 30 minutes. Preheat the oven to 500 degrees.

On a floured work surface, roll out the dough into a 12-inch circle and place on a pizza pan or peel that has been lightly sprinkled with a little cornmeal. Brush the edge of the crust with the warm honey and spoon the tamarillo purée over the top of the pizza, except for the edges. Bake the pizza in the oven for 8 minutes.

Remove the pizza and sprinkle the salsa topping and mint leaves evenly over the tamarillo purée. Dollop the mascarpone or ricotta in small spoonfuls over the pizza and return to the oven for 1 or 2 minutes.

Remove the pizza from the oven and let rest for 1 or 2 minutes, to set. Cut into slices and serve.

Yield: 4 to 6 servings

RUM CARAMEL-ESPRESSO POACHED "NIÑO" BANANA SPLITS

Names abound, but the fruit remains the same. The little, fat, sweet banana I like to use in this recipe is also known as the apple banana, lady finger banana, *manzano,* or *datil.* The key is to let the banana get fully ripe. Any leftovers can be cut up and folded into a pancake or waffle batter.

7 tablespoons hot water

½ cup sugar

½ teaspoon fresh lemon juice

2 teaspoons *añejo* (aged) rum

¼ cup freshly brewed espresso coffee

6 Niño (finger) bananas, peeled and split lengthwise

In a heavy saucepan, combine 2 tablespoons of the hot water with the sugar and cook over medium-high heat, stirring occasionally, until golden brown. Very carefully whisk in the remaining 5 tablespoons of hot water—be prepared for it to spatter. Add the lemon juice, rum, and espresso, return to a boil, and then turn off the heat.

Put the bananas in a saucepan and cover with the prepared poaching caramel. Cover the mixture with a piece of parchment paper cut to size and poach over medium heat until the liquid has turned syrupy and the bananas are soft, about 10 to 14 minutes, depending on the ripeness of the bananas. Transfer to serving dishes and top with your choice of ice cream, nuts, fruits, and chocolate sauce.

Yield: 6 servings

CREAMY, BUT FROZEN PASSION

This is a striking presentation that is enhanced by edible flowers set on the bed of crushed ice in each serving bowl.

6 to 8 passion fruits

½ cup sugar

3 extra large egg yolks

2 extra large egg whites

½ cup heavy cream, chilled

Cut the passion fruits in half, scrape out the seeds and juice, and reserve the shells. Strain the seeds and reserve the juice (you will need ⅔ cup). Cut a thin layer off the bottom of the shells so they will stand upright. Wrap the sides with masking tape for a clean presentation.

Cut parchment paper into 12 strips, about 6 inches by 2½ inches, depending on the size of the passion fruits. Tightly wrap a strip around each half shell and tape closed so a 1-inch collar stands above the rim of the shell. Set each passion fruit half in the mold of a muffin pan.

In a stainless steel bowl, blend together the sugar, egg yolks and the ⅓ cup of strained passion fruit juice. Bring a saucepan of water almost to a boil and set the bowl over the saucepan; the bottom of the bowl should not be touching the water. Whisk the egg mixture constantly until the temperature reaches 160 degrees. Remove the bowl from the heat and continue to whisk until the mixture has cooled and is pale yellow in color. In a separate bowl, whisk the cream to soft peaks. Fold in the passion fruit mixture until well blended. In another bowl, whisk the egg whites to stiff peaks and fold into the passion fruit cream.

Spoon about ¼ to ⅓ cup of this mixture into each prepared passion fruit shell, and freeze. When ready to serve, remove the parchment paper collars and masking tape. Serve 2 or 3 passion fruit halves per person (depending on the size of the passion fruits), set in the middle of chilled serving bowls on a bed of crushed ice.

Yield: 4 to 6 servings

CANISTEL "EGG NOG" ICE CREAM

This ice cream is a great medium for the egg-like richness of the canistel, or yellow sapote.

½ nutmeg

1 cinnamon stick

⅔ cup sugar

1 vanilla bean, split in half lengthwise

3 cups heavy cream

9 extra large egg yolks

1 cup strained ripe canistel purée

Break the nutmeg and cinnamon into smaller pieces. Grind in a spice grinder and set aside. Sprinkle a tablespoon of the sugar on a cutting board. Scrape out the vanilla bean seeds onto the sugar and smear around to separate the seeds. In a saucepan, heat the cream, half of the remaining sugar, the sugar mixed with the vanilla seeds, the ground nutmeg and cinnamon, and the vanilla bean pod. Stir occasionally until just boiling.

Combine the egg yolks and remaining sugar in a mixing bowl. Slowly whisk in some of the hot cream mixture and return to the saucepan. Continue to cook over low heat, stirring constantly, until the mixture thickens enough to coat the back of a spoon, about 1 to 2 minutes.

Remove from the heat and let cool. Chill in the refrigerator, stirring occasionally. Remove the vanilla bean pod. Whisk in the canistel purée and transfer to an ice cream machine. Freeze according to the manufacturer's instructions.

Yield: 5 to 6 cups

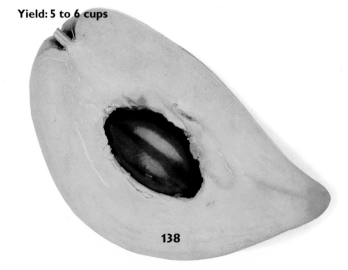

✦ ✦ ✦

MANGO CINNAMON SORBET

You start this sorbet by making a cinnamon-infused simple syrup. It is very easy, and I encourage you to create infusions made with other spices or herbs to accompany other fruit—there's a world of opportunity out there! You can keep the leftover syrup for weeks in the refrigerator.

FOR THE CINNAMON SIMPLE SYRUP:

- $\frac{1}{4}$ **cup water**
- $\frac{1}{4}$ **cup sugar**
- **I stick cinnamon**

FOR THE SORBET:

- **2$\frac{1}{2}$ cups puréed, strained fresh mango (2 to 3 fresh mangoes)**
- $\frac{1}{4}$ **cup fresh pineapple juice**
- $\frac{1}{4}$ **cup fresh lime juice**
- **Freshly ground cinnamon, to taste**

To prepare the syrup, whisk together the water and sugar in a saucepan. Add the cinnamon stick, bring to a boil, and turn off the heat. Let the mixture steep for 30 minutes. Strain and reserve the syrup.

Transfer $\frac{1}{4}$ cup of the syrup to a mixing bowl. Add the puréed mango, pineapple juice, and lime juice, and mix together. Transfer this mixture to an ice cream machine and freeze according to the manufacturer's directions. Serve in small, chilled dishes and sprinkle with the ground cinnamon.

Yield: About one quart

CANDIED KUMQUAT KEY LIME PIE

The first time I saw a Key lime pie was a few days after I started a new job in 1973 as the midnight-to-dawn shift cook in an all-night place in Key West. It was about 8 A.M. and I was having a cold beer, reading yesterday's *Citizen,* and getting ready to go home to bed. Just then a young lady named Sunshine walked in, wearing a large hibiscus flower behind her left ear, bearing a large tray containing two pale yellow pies. She explained that she only prepared two at a time; besides, she only had room for two in her bicycle basket. I ran into Sunshine a dozen years later: she had become Jimmy Buffet's business manager but *still* made only two pies at a time. I'm only going to make one here (I don't have a basket on my bicycle). The kumquats are optional and the recipe will work without them, but they help cut the sweetness down in what, ordinarily, is nearly a deathly-sweet dessert.

FOR THE CRUST:

- **1 cup graham cracker crumbs**
- **½ cup toasted and ground almonds, or nuts of your choice**
- **3 tablespoons sugar**
- **1 teaspoon ground cinnamon**
- **1 teaspoon ground nutmeg**
- **¼ cup melted butter**

◆ ◆ ◆

6 extra large egg yolks

2 cups sweetened condensed milk

**¹⁄₄ cup candied kumquats (recipe follows),
seeds and pulp discarded, finely chopped**

1³⁄₄ cups fresh Key lime juice

Preheat the oven to 375 degrees. Combine all
the crust ingredients in a mixing bowl and press
firmly into the bottom of a 10-inch pie pan, and
up the sides.

In another mixing bowl, whisk the egg yolks
until thick and pale yellow, about 5 minutes. Pour
in the condensed milk and kumquats. Slowly add
the lime juice, while whisking.

Pour the filling into the crust and bake in the
oven for 10 to 12 minutes. Remove from the oven
and cool for 1 hour. Chill in the refrigerator.

Yield: One 10-inch pie

CANDIED KUMQUATS

10 kumquats

²⁄₃ cup sugar

¹⁄₃ cup fresh orange juice

Place the kumquats in a heavy saucepan and
cover with water. Bring to a boil over high heat,
and drain. Transfer the kumquats to a bowl of ice
water and let cool.

Drain the kumquats, place on a cutting board,
and trim both ends. Bring the sugar and orange
juice to a boil in a saucepan, lower the heat to a
simmer, and add the fruit. Simmer for 50 to 60
minutes, stirring occasionally to make sure the fruit
is not sticking to the bottom of the pan. Remove
the kumquats and reserve on a plate lined with
parchment paper.

WEST INDIAN PUMPKIN POUND CAKE WITH A MONSTERA MASH ANGLAISE

The ideal Halloween dessert! It is delicious with any number of fruits replacing the monstera in the *anglaise*—such as banana, mango, pineapple, papaya, or Asian pear.

FOR THE ANGLAISE:

½ vanilla bean, split in half lengthwise

5 tablespoons sugar

I cup heavy cream

2 extra large egg yolks

¾ cup monstera fruit, lightly mashed

FOR THE POUND CAKE:

1¼ pounds West Indian pumpkin (calabaza), peeled and cut into I inch dice

2 cups all-purpose flour

½ teaspoon baking powder

½ teaspoon salt

8 ounces butter

1¼ cups sugar

5 extra large eggs

2 teaspoons pure vanilla extract

2 tablespoons dark rum

To prepare the anglaise, scrape out the vanilla bean seeds onto 1 tablespoon of the sugar and smear around to separate the seeds. Transfer to a saucepan and add the cream and 2 more tablespoons of the sugar. Bring to a scald (or just below boiling) over

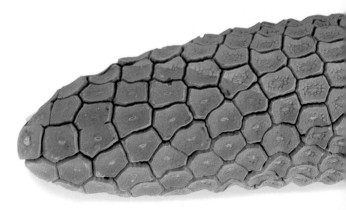

medium-high heat, and then turn down the heat to medium.

Meanwhile, in a mixing bowl, slowly whisk together the egg yolks and the remaining 2 tablespoons of sugar. Add some of the hot cream mixture while whisking constantly, and then return this mixture to the saucepan, while stirring. Cook while stirring with a wooden spoon until the mixture thickens enough to coat the back of the spoon.

Place the monstera in a mixing bowl and strain the anglaise over it. Stir together, cover, and reserve in the refrigerator for at least 1 hour for the flavors to intensify.

To prepare the pound cake, place the pumpkin in a large saucepan and cover with water. Simmer over medium heat until soft, about 10 to 15 minutes. Drain and place in a mixing bowl. Mash well and set aside.

Preheat the oven to 350 degrees. Butter and lightly flour a 9 x 5 x 3-inch baking pan. Sift the flour, baking powder, and salt into a bowl. In a mixer, beat the butter until fluffy. Add the sugar and beat well. Add the eggs, one at a time, and beat for about 5 minutes or until the mixture is light in color. Add the pumpkin, vanilla, and rum, and beat in. Add the flour mixture and beat until just mixed. Pour the batter into the loaf pan.

Bake the batter in the oven for $1\frac{1}{4}$ hours. Remove and let cool to room temperature. Turn out onto a cutting board or plate and serve with the reserved anglaise.

Yield: One 9-inch cake

SOURCES

Brooks Tropicals
P.O. Box 900160
Homestead, FL 33090
800-327-4833

Frieda's Finest
P.O. Box 58488
Los Angeles, CA 90058

Garden of Earthly Delights
14560 S.W. 14th Street
Davie, FL 33325

LNB Groves
25250 S.W. 194th Avenue
Homestead, FL 33031

Possum Trot Tropical Fruit
  Nursery
14955 S.W. 214th Street
Miami, FL 33187

Robert Is Here
34815 S.W. 202nd Avenue
Homestead, FL 33034

W. O. Lessard
19201 S.W. 248th Street
Homestead, FL 33031

CONVERSIONS

For cooks outside the United States, here are some equivalent ingredients and measurements:

all-purpose flour	plain flour
bell pepper	sweet pepper, capsicum
cilantro	fresh coriander
cornmeal	ground corn, maize
heavy cream	double cream
honey	clear honey
papaya	pawpaw
red onion	Italian onion
yellow onion	Spanish onion

DRY WEIGHT:

30 g = 1 oz.

120 g = 4 oz. = $\frac{1}{4}$ lb.

250 g = 8 oz. = $\frac{1}{2}$ lb.

500 g = 16 oz. = 1 lb.

LIQUID MEASUREMENTS:

$\frac{1}{4}$ cup = 60 mL = 2 fl. oz.

$\frac{1}{3}$ cup = 80 mL = 3 fl. oz.

$\frac{1}{2}$ cup = 120 mL = 4 fl. oz.

$\frac{3}{4}$ cup = 180 mL = 6 fl. oz.

1 cup = 250 mL = 8 fl. oz.

$1\frac{1}{2}$ cups = 375 mL = 12 fl. oz.

SOME SAMPLE EQUIVALENTS:

butter	1 cup = 250 g = 8 oz.
coconut, dried	1 cup = 90 g = 3 oz
couscous	1 cup = 220 g = 7 oz.
flour	1 cup = 155 g = 5 oz.
fresh fruit, chopped	1 cup = 120 g = 4 oz.
goat cheese	1 cup = 120 g = 4 oz.
honey, molasses, etc.	1 cup = 375 g = 12 oz.
nuts, chopped	1 cup = 120 g = 4 oz.
sugar (granulated)	1 cup = 250 g = 8 oz.
sugar, brown (firmly packed)	1 cup = 185 g = 6 oz.

INDEX

A

Acerola, 6
Akee, 6
Alligator pear. *See* Avocado
Ancho Chile and Guava Glazed
    Smoked Ham, 106–7
Apple pear. *See* Pear, Asian
Arroz con Coco Oriente, 124
Atemoya, 8
Avocado
    about, 10
    Bajan Avocado Cocktail Salsa,
        111
    Cherimoya-Avocado Salad,
        94–95

B

Babaco, 12
Bahama Mama Mamey Milk
    Shake, 83
Bajan Avocado Cocktail
    Salsa, 111
Banana. *See also* Plantain
    about, 14
    Batido Exótico, 82
    finger, 14
    Fish and Fruit "Port of
        Call," 102–3
    Jamaican Banana-Pineapple
        Rum Bread, 130
    Jamaican Red Banana and
        Peanut Fritters, 92–93
    red, 14
    Rum Caramel-Espresso
        Poached "Niño" Banana
        Splits, 136
Barbados cherry. *See* Acerola
Batido Exótico, 82
Bergamot. *See* Orange, sour
Beverages
    Bahama Mama Mamey Milk
        Shake, 83
    Batido Exótico, 82
    Puckery Prickly Pear
        Limeade, 81
    Sapodilla Root Beer Float, 88
    Shocking Pink Limeade, 80
    Sun-Burned Rum Runner,
        86–87
    Tamarind Twister, 84
    Tropical Black Cow, 88
Bigarade. *See* Orange, sour
Bignay, 16
Bread, Jamaican Banana-Pine-
    apple Rum, 130
Breadfruit, 18
Breadfruit, Mexican.
    See Monstera

C

Cactus pear. *See* Prickly pear
Calomondin, 18
Canistel
    about, 20
    Canistel "Egg Nog" Ice
        Cream, 138
Carambola. *See* Star fruit
Ceriman. *See* Monstera
Cherimoya
    about, 20
    Cherimoya-Avocado Salad,
        94–95
    Exotic Fruits Curry, 112–13
Chinese gooseberry.
    See Kiwi fruit
Chinese pear. *See* Pear, Asian
Chocolate pudding fruit.
    See Sapote, black
Ciruela, 22
Citron, 22
Clementine, 22
Coconut
    about, 24
    Arroz con Coco
        Oriente, 124
    East Indian Spiced Fruit
        Yogurt, 117
Coffee, 24
Condiments
    East Indian Spiced Fruit
        Yogurt, 117
    Homemade Key Lime
        Mustard, 119
    Horned Melon Raita, 118
    Mango-Tamarind Ketchup,
        122–23
    Pawpaw Pickle Tartar Relish,
        114–15
    Pepino, Mango, and Asian
        Pear Slaw, 116
    Pineapple and Sugarcane
        Moonshine Chutney, 120
    Sweet and Sour
        Jaboticabas, 115
Couscous, Pummelo Juice, 125
Creamy *But Frozen* Passion, 137
Curry, Exotic Fruits, 112–13
Custard apple. *See* Cherimoya

D

Date, 26
Datil. *See* Banana
Desserts
    Candied Kumquat Key Lime
        Pie, 140–41
    Canistel "Egg Nog" Ice
        Cream, 138

Creamy *But Frozen*
    Passion, 137
Pie, 131
Fruit Salsa Speckled Sweet
    Pizza Pie, 134–35
Mango Cinnamon
    Sorbet, 139
Rum Caramel-Espresso
    Poached "Niño" Banana
    Splits, 136
West Indian Pumpkin Pound
    Cake, 142–43
Dragon's eye. *See* Longan
Durian, 26

E

East Indian Spiced Fruit
    Yogurt, 117
Egg fruit. *See* Canistel

F

Feijoa, 28
Fig
    about, 28
    East Indian Spiced Fruit
        Yogurt, 117
Fish and Fruit "Port of
    Call," 102–3
Flapjacks, Star Fruit, 128
French Fries, Tropical
    Tuber, 122–23
Fritters, Jamaican Red Banana
    and Peanut, 92–93
Fruit, mixed
    Chilled Exotic Fruit
        Soup, 90–91
    Double Fruit Cocktail
        "Straight Up," 91
    East Indian Spiced Fruit
        Yogurt, 117
    Exotic Fruits Curry, 112–13
    Sweet Pizza Pie, 134–35
    Mixed Greens and Fruits
        Salad, 96–97
    Preserve of Six Citrus
        Fruits with Five Spice
        Powder, 85
Fruta bomba. *See* Papaya

G

Grape, muscadine, 52
Grapefruit, 30
Guanabana
    about, 30
    Hot Guanabana-Lime Soufflé,
        132–33
Guava
    about, 32
    Ancho Chile and Guava
        Glazed Smoked Ham,
        106–7
Guava, pineapple. *See* Feijoa

H

Ham, Ancho Chile and Guava
    Glazed Smoked, 106–7
Horned melon. *See* Kiwano

I

Ice cream
    Bahama Mama Mamey Milk
        Shake, 83
    Canistel "Egg Nog" Ice
        Cream, 138
Imbé, 32

J

Jaboticaba
    about, 34
    Sweet and Sour
        Jaboticabas, 115
Jakfruit, 34
Jamaican Banana-Pineapple Rum
    Bread, 130
Jamaican Red Banana and Peanut
    Fritters, 92–93
Java apple. *See* Wax jambu

K

Ketchup, Mango-Tamarind,
    122–23
Key West Plantain Stuffed and
    Spiced Pork Tenderloin,
    100–101
Kiwano
    about, 36
    Horned Melon Raita, 118
Kiwi fruit, 36
Kumquat
    about, 38
    Candied Kumquat Key Lime
        Pie, 140–41

L

Lamb Chops, Pomegranate
    Molasses Marinated and
    Grilled, 104–5
Langsat, 38
Lemon, 38
Lime
    about, 40
    Candied Kumquat Key Lime
        Pie, 140–41
    Homemade Key Lime
        Mustard, 119
    Hot Guanabana-Lime Soufflé,
        132–33
    Puckery Prickly Pear
        Limeade, 81
    Shocking Pink Limeade, 80
Lime, Spanish. *See* Mamoncillo
Longan, 42
Lychee, 42

M

Mabolo. See Velvet apple
Macaboo. See Banana
Macadamia nut, 44
Mamey sapote
    about, 44
    Bahama Mama Mamey Milk
        Shake, 83
    Mamey Sapote and Cuban
        Sweet Potato Waffles, 129
Mamoncillo, 46
Mandarin orange.
        See Clementine
Mango
    about, 46
    Batido Exótico, 82
    East Indian Spiced Fruit
        Yogurt, 117
    Exotic Fruits Curry, 112–13
    Fish and Fruit "Port of
        Call," 102–3
    Mango Cinnamon
        Sorbet, 139
    Pepino, Mango, and Asian
        Pear Slaw, 116
    Pineapple and Sugarcane
        Moonshine Chutney, 120
    Tropical Tuber French Fries
        and Mango-Tamarind
        Ketchup, 122–23
Mangosteen, 48
Matasano. See Sapote, white
Melon, Charantais or French, 48
Melon, horned. See Kiwano
Melon pear. See Pepino
Mexican breadfruit.
        See Monstera
Miracle fruit, 50
Monstera
    about, 50
    West Indian Pumpkin Pound
        Cake, 142–43
Morado. See Banana
Mountain papaya. See Babaco
Mustard, Homemade Key
        Lime, 119

N

Nashi. See Pear, Asian
Nispero. See Sapodilla

O

Orange, mandarin.
        See Clementine
Orange, sour
    about, 68
    Key West Plantain Stuffed
        and Spiced Pork Tender-
        loin, 100–101

P

Papaya
    about, 54
    All-Purpose Exotic Fruit
        Salsa, 110
    Batido Exótico, 82
    East Indian Spiced Fruit
        Yogurt, 117
    Exotic Fruits Curry, 112–13
    Fish and Fruit "Port of
        Call," 102–3
    green, 54
    Pawpaw Pickle Tartar
        Relish, 114–15
    Pineapple and Sugarcane
        Moonshine Chutney, 120
Papaya, mountain. See Babaco
Passion fruit
    about, 56
    Cherimoya-Avocado Salad,
        94–95
    Creamy But Frozen Passion,
        137
Pawpaw. See Papaya
Peanut butter fruit. See Ciruela
Pear, Asian
    about, 8
    Deep Dish Asian Pear
        Pie, 131
    Pepino, Mango, and Asian
        Pear Slaw, 116
Pepino
    about, 58
    Pepino, Mango, and Asian
        Pear Slaw, 116
Persimmon, 58
Persimmon, black. See Sapote,
        black
Pineapple
    about, 60
    All-Purpose Exotic Fruit
        Salsa, 110
    Batido Exótico, 82
    Double Fruit Cocktail
        "Straight Up," 91
    East Indian Spiced Fruit
        Yogurt, 117
    Jamaican Banana-Pineapple
        Rum Bread, 130
    Pineapple and Sugarcane
        Moonshine Chutney, 120
    Pineapple–Scotch Bonnet
        Mojo, 113
Pineapple guava. See Feijoa
Pizza Pie, Fruit Salsa Speckled
        Sweet, 134–35
Plantain
    about, 62
    East Indian Spiced Fruit
        Yogurt, 117
    Hawaiian, 62

Key West Plantain Stuffed
and Spiced Pork Tender-
loin, 100–101
Pomegranate
about, 64
Pomegranate Molasses
Marinated and Grilled
Lamb Chops, 104–5
Sun-Burned Rum Runner,
86–87
Pomelo. See Pummelo
Pork
Ancho Chile and Guava
Glazed Smoked Ham,
106–7
Key West Plantain Stuffed
and Spiced Pork Tender-
loin, 100–101
Preserve of Six Citrus
Fruits with Five Spice
Powder, 85
Prickly pear
about, 64
Puckery Prickly Pear
Limeade, 81
Shocking Pink Limeade, 80
Pummelo
about, 66
Pummelo Juice
Couscous, 125

R

Rambutan, 66
Relishes. See Condiments
Rice, 124
Rum Caramel-Espresso Poached
"Niño" Banana Splits, 136

S

Salads
Cherimoya-Avocado
Salad, 94–95
Mixed Greens and Fruits
Salad, 96–97
Salsas and sauces
All-Purpose Exotic Fruit
Salsa, 110
Bajan Avocado Cocktail
Salsa, 111
Exotic Fruits Curry, 112–13
Fruit Salsa Speckled Sweet
Pizza Pie, 134–35
Pineapple–Scotch Bonnet
Mojo, 113
Sand pear. See Pear, Asian
Sapodilla
about, 68
Sapodilla Root Beer Float, 88
Sapote, black, 16
Sapote, mamey. See Mamey
sapote

Sapote, white
about, 76
Exotic Fruits Curry, 112–13
Sapote, yellow. See Canistel
Shaddock. See Pummelo
Sorbet, Mango Cinnamon, 139
Soufflé, Hot Guanabana-Lime,
132–33
Soup, Chilled Exotic Fruit, 90–91
Soursop. See Guanabana
Spanish lime. See Mamoncillo
Star fruit
about, 70
Star Fruit Flapjacks, 128
Sugar apple, 70
Sun-Burned Rum Runner, 86–87
Sweetsop. See Sugar apple

T

Tamarillo
about, 72
Exotic Fruits Curry, 112–13
Fruit Salsa Speckled Sweet
Pizza Pie, 134–35
Tamarind
about, 72
Exotic Fruits Curry, 112–13
Tamarind Twister, 84
Tropical Tuber French Fries
and Mango-Tamarind
Ketchup, 122–23
Tangelo, ugli. See Unique fruit
Tree melon. See Papaya; Pepino
Tree tomato. See Tamarillo
Tropical Black Cow, 88
Tropical Tuber French Fries
and Mango-Tamarind
Ketchup, 122–23
Tuna. See Prickly pear

U, V

Ugli tangelo, 74
Unique fruit, 74
Velvet apple, 74

W

Waffles, Mamey Sapote and
Cuban Sweet Potato, 129
Wampi, 76
Wax jambu, 76
West Indian Pumpkin Pound
Cake, 142–43

Y

Yogurt
East Indian Spiced Fruit
Yogurt, 117
Horned Melon Raita, 118

MORE EXOTIC FRUIT...

THE EXOTIC FRUIT POSTERS

These lovely, high-quality posters measure 24 x 36 inches, and add zest to any wall—kitchen, kids' room, breakfast nook, or elsewhere in the home. Divided into tropical and subtropical fruits, each

features color repro-ductions accompanied by brief descriptions, making them not only beautiful, but informa-tional as well. When ordering, specify whether you want tropical, subtropical, or both.

EXOTIC FRUIT POSTCARDS

This little gem spotlights 24 of the most attractive or unusual fruits from this book on tear-out, ready-to-mail postcards. Just the thing for con-

veying sweet nothings or juicy gossip, or for use as small decorative elements in home or office.

For more information, or to order, call the publisher at the number below. We accept VISA, Mastercard, and American Express. You may also wish to write for our free catalog of over 500 books, posters, and audiotapes.

TEN SPEED PRESS 800-841-BOOK
P.O. BOX 7123 · BERKELEY, CA 94707